WITNESSING MADE EASY

THE LADDER-METHOD

WITNESSING IS NOT WINNING

Soul-winning and witnessing are NOT the same. While everyone can witness for Jesus, not everyone can win souls—at least not at first.

I was in an evangelical church bringing a series on witnessing. At the end of the first lecture a tearful lady hurried forward to speak to me. She was nervous and perspiring. Her hands kept tearing at a knotted hand-kerchief:

"Dr. Lovett, I'm ashamed to say this, but I just can't witness for the Lord. I don't know how to win souls. I've never had any kind of training and I'm so scared, I'm afraid to try."

"**Forget soul-winning,**" I said to her. "**Put it out of your mind. I'm not going to ask you or anyone else in this class to win souls. This is a course on witnessing, not soul-winning.**"

The moment she heard I wasn't expecting her to win souls, her shoulders dropped in relief. Like many others, she thought she couldn't be a witness for the Lord without being a soul-winner. When I explained the difference between winning and witnessing, joy brightened her face. Her fear of soul-winning had so blinded her mind, she hadn't grasped one of the techniques I demonstrated in the first session.

So I took a moment and gave her some **easy** helps for getting started as a witness. She went away rejoicing. She was ready now to get serious about witnessing. But as long as she thought witnessing meant winning souls, she was too terrified to learn anything. Until that night she didn't realize there was an easy way to get started in the business of reaching others for Jesus.

The Lord Jesus installed the witnessing program to accomodate this variable in His people. Everyone can begin with the easiest steps, and then, with the passing of time, graduate to harder ones.

The Holy Spirit has a treat for those who will let a word of witness come from their mouths. There is an adventure in power for those who will let their light shine. And it is easier than you would ever suspect.

THIS BOOK TELLS HOW!

WITNESSING MADE EASY

THE LADDER-METHOD

by C. S. LOVETT

M. A., M. Div., Ph. D.

President of Personal Christianity

author of
"HELP LORD—THE DEVIL WANTS ME FAT!"
SOUL-WINNING MADE EASY
DEALING WITH THE DEVIL
LATEST WORD ON THE LAST DAYS
LONGING TO BE LOVED

Illustrated by Marjorie Lovett
and Linda Lovett

Published and Distributed
by

PERSONAL CHRISTIANITY

Baldwin Park, California

PRINTED IN THE UNITED STATES OF AMERICA

ISBN 0-938148-01-X

CONTENTS

DEDICATED TO

The *HOLY SPIRIT*

For His generosity in granting the
anointing and insights needed
to bring this work to His people.
And upon Whom these very
words depend for a witness to
the reader's heart.

A SHOCK FOR CHRIST!

"Hey! You @$%&¢* kids keep away from there!"

It hurt me to hear those words, and it hurts me to think of them now. But that's the way a cement finisher shouted at two boys playing near his newly poured driveway.

"$%&@=¢ Almighty, I get a job done and then some damn kids come along and mess it up." He was expressing himself with typical profanity. But he wasn't ready for my comment:

"Why don't you try your mother's name?"

"Huh?" He jerked. "What are you talking about?"

"I see you use people's names when you get mad. It was just a suggestion. Maybe you'd feel better if you swore with her name. But I doubt if she'd like it any better than God does."

You should have seen the consternation on his face! His next words were a crude apology. "I didn't mean anything by it. I was just letting off steam. I'm sorry."

"You don't have to apologize to me. It wasn't my name you used. If you want forgiveness, you'll have to ask God, not me." That did it. The door was wide open for a testimony about the forgiveness I had received, and I knew personally that the Lord would be very happy to forgive him **if he would ask.**

● Now you can say that was rough treatment for a man who was simply swearing out of habit with no thought of defaming the Lord. For there he was, bewildered by what had just happened. Out of a clear blue sky he had been faced with the matter of his offense to God. You couldn't help but feel sorry for him. The Holy Spirit was really using the situation to press home the witness.

7

That is the power of know-how! A few words and a man can be caused to stop in his tracks and ponder his condition before God. When Christians use this kind of know-how, in cooperation with the Holy Spirit, the effect is tremendous. Picture yourself equipped with the know-how for dealing with a multitude of situations like the one just mentioned. And at the same time imagine yourself skilled in the science of working with the Holy Spirit at **close range!** Why, you could move among men with such power that your entire life would be a shock for Christ.

THAT IS WHAT THIS BOOK CAN MEAN TO YOU!

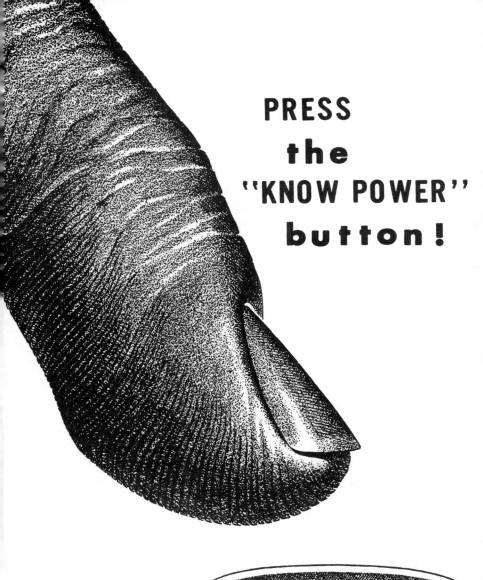

PRESS
the
"KNOW POWER"
button!

"GO YE"

Chapter One

DANGER IN THE DARK

One very black night, during World War II, I was making my way from a section of Karachi, India, to the officers' club. I had left my buddies in the city and was walking by myself when a beggar approached my side.

"Bak-shees, Sahib, bak-shees." You hear this continually on the streets of India where begging is a profession. Foreigners are plagued with that cry for money.

"Nay mallum . . . Jao!" I replied. I had gotten used to brushing off beggars.

But he was persistent. Again and again he begged, and it seemed he kept getting closer all the time. It was pitch dark, and I could just barely make out his form, but I could feel his breath near my neck. And that's close.

Ahead was a peanut vendor's wagon and a little gas flame provided a ring of light. As we neared the illuminated circle, I could begin to see the man at my side. But then I saw some-

 thing else—and it turned my heart to ice! It was not the man's breath I was feeling, but that of a huge python which he carried coiled about his body. He was holding the head of that ugly reptile close to the side of my face. I was terrified.

Did I give him money? You bet. What a relief to see him go away. I had just received a lesson in extortion, but even more significant I had met the real danger of darkness. I was in danger and **didn't know it.** It wasn't until a wee bit of light revealed my peril that I saw the threat and did something about it.

What of the multitudes about us? Is not their spiritual darkness more dreadful than the fangs of a python? No wonder God asks His people to shine for Him when even the tiniest flicker can expose a man to his peril? What shame then must belong to that Christian who withholds his light from his neighbor? And what will be the Lord's charge against those who refuse even the faintest glimmer that a lost one might see his peril and do something about it?

FLICKER?

> "I don't believe we should go around talking about religion. I just let my light shine. People know where I stand."

Have you ever heard that? Of course you have. That particular phrase has been used and used until it is now one of the saddest of our Christian expressions. What does it mean?

It means that the speaker deems it unnecessary to say one word about Christ outside the church. He figures if he follows a certain pattern of life, the unsaved who observe his life will be impressed to the place where they will come seeking Christ. Now some who say that are quite sincere. But usually it **is an excuse.**

The hurtful fact is that a wonderful Scripture has been twisted to justify the action. One of the sweetest things Jesus taught His disciples upon the Mount is used as an excuse for **disobedience.** Here is His Word:

> "Let your light so shine before men, that they may see your good works and glorify your Father which is in heaven" (Matt. 5:16).

This is a definite instruction. A second look at it might rescue someone from awful deception. Satan has used this precious verse to silence many of God's people by giving it a slight twist. But that's his way, isn't it?

11

LIGHT

Light is so blessed. Those who lose their sight really know how blessed. But we get a taste when we walk into a dark room. There is an unsafe feeling, and our feet cautiously explore ahead for unseen objects and pieces of furniture. We listen for the sound of any lurking person. Hastily we grope for the switch. Ah . . . what a relief. That comforting light floods the room, and we see everything in its place.

 Light is so good. It explains everything around. We walk without fear through crowded stores and work around busy machines. We drive midst speeding free-way traffic. We go swiftly and directly because we can see where we're going and what is to be avoided. Yes, light, whether from a bulb or from the sun, makes it possible to come and go with ease. Without it, life can be dangerous.

Now we are ready to see why God's Word is called light. The Psalmist mentions it this way:

"The entrance of thy words giveth light" (Psa. 119:130).

and again,

"Thy word is a lamp unto my feet and a light unto my path" (Psa. 119:105).

The Word of God shines. Just as the sun scatters physical darkness, so does the Bible illuminate men. Without God's Word, men cannot see. They have no way of determining their direction, **spiritually.** They don't know where they have come from or where they are going. They cannot even explain **who they are.**

I won't forget a comment made by the actor Marlon Brando during the filming of "The Ugly American." As he came out

12

of the studio commissary, the reporter, Peer Oppenheimer, asked:

"Marlon, how are you today?"

"I don't know," was the answer. "I don't even know **who** I am." And it's true. Until men are able to view life under the light of God's Word, they cannot even understand themselves let alone the world in which they live. They are in the dark. The Bible is a huge street light that shines upon the world. See it by this holy light, and it makes sense. Without it, the human story is meaningless. The point of what I am saying is that

GOD'S WORD IS HIS LIGHT!

YOUR LIGHT

"Let your light shine . . ." says Jesus. What is your light? Your light is **your word** and it can shine on your works, just as God's light shines on His works. You see, men can marvel at the works of God and give Him no credit. When He does something wonderful in your life, men can see it and give you the credit instead of God. They will never give Him credit for anything in your life, **unless you direct their attention to Him.**

The sun comes up every morning, and men never think to credit the One Who made it and sees that it maintains its schedule. If men can behold a dazzling wonder that fills the sky and fail to recognize our God, they will surely never credit Him with a small wonder in your life—**unless you say so.**

"Let your light (words) so shine . . . men can see your good works and credit God for them." Notice in my paraphrase that your **light** and your **works** are two separate things? Your light has nothing to do with your works. Your light merely illuminates your works to reveal that they are wrought in God. And God's Light has nothing to do with His works

13

either. His works and His Light are two separate things. But without His Light, men do not see that they are His. And without your light, men will never see His hand in your life. That's the point.

IT'S LIKE THIS

I once had a dear friend whose wife was hospitalized with polio. For eight years she lay in an iron lung until God released her from that prison of flesh. Faithfully, three times a week, year in and year out, that precious brother would visit her. People saw his faithfulness and said, "Oh, isn't he a good man!" Besides that, he did a great job in caring for the children by himself. He gave them discipline and Christian teaching. People saw this too and said, "Oh, isn't he a wonderful father!"

His language was pure and he refused to speak evil against anyone. He was faithful in serving his church and again they noted, "What a fine man he is." And He was a fine man. He truly loved the Lord and was able to endure these hardships because the Lord stood by him. But the people saw only my friend and his devotion to his family and the church. They didn't even consider that it was Jesus Who made it possible. They thought, "What a wonderful person he is. I could never do that!"

You tell me who got the credit, who got the praise? The people saw his good works, but who did they glorify? They marvelled at my brother, but they did not glorify his Father which is in heaven. And why not? His light was not shining. There were no **words** to **illuminate** the gracious works and indicate that God was responsible for them. Until he would open his mouth and credit the Lord openly, no one was about to acknowledge the goodness of our Savior.

14

Then we had a little talk. At once he saw the difference between his works and his words (light). He began to open his mouth. After that everyone who commented on his good works learned from him that it was Jesus who made it all possible. He became a powerful witness. A new stream of comment arose,

**"If the Lord can do that for Mr. . . . ,
He can surely do it for me."**

Many people were attracted to the grace of the Lord Jesus Christ, because of the **word** of this man. But it wasn't until he began to speak that the Lord received the glory. My dear brother learned that his light was his word.

● Dr. Samuel Shoemaker once said, "I can't by being good tell of Jesus' atoning death and resurrection nor of my faith in Him, because the emphasis would be too much on me and too little on Him."

THE UNOPENED CASE

"I just let my light shine. People see me carry my Bible to church. That's enough. They know where I stand. I'm not called to deal with them."

Now imagine a doctor saying something like that. Watch him as he enters the hospital. He goes from room to room with a big smile on his face and a sweet hello for everyone. From his right hand hangs a medical bag. Everyone knows by that he's a doctor. But he is a different kind of doctor. He never opens that bag. No medicine or help ever comes from the kit. What kind of a doctor is that, do you suppose? Let's ask him:

"Doctor, how come you never open your bag and give any medicine to the people?"

15

> "Oh, I'm not called to do that. I just want people to know that I am a doctor. They'll see my bag and know that I am a physician. That's enough to make them well."

That's ridiculous, you say. Of course it is—when we talk about a doctor. But is it any less ridiculous when applied to the Christian? What about the one who is identified with the Word of God and never opens it? Is there any difference between a Christian who will not open his mouth and a doctor who will not open his case?

WITNESSING MAGIC

One day I was shopping for machine parts to fix a piece of equipment here at Personal Christianity. The salesman in the supply house was a rough character who added equal parts of profanity to his English. I located a couple of possible items. He was watching me, and I studied his face as I made the next remark:

> "The Lord will have to show me which one of these to take. I just can't seem to decide which one I really need."

The effect was magical. His manner completely changed. The voice softened and the profanity disappeared. The testimony was there in the form of announced dependence upon the Lord. And it was as though Jesus had walked on the scene. I saw a hostile and coarse man revamp his personality in a split-second. It was almost funny. What strange power goes with witnessing.

Did you ever watch kids cutting up while the teacher is out of the room? And just the moment she walks back through that door they become little angels? The world has the feeling the Lord is nowhere in sight and when you mention Him, the situation is electric. There is power in that name. But it is manifested **only when spoken.** Speak out to identify yourself with Christ and see God's power. The Holy Spirit has a treat for those who will let a word of witness come from their mouths. There is an adventure in power for those who will let their light shine. And it is easier than you would ever suspect.

Some of that easing—next.

Chapter Two

WITNESSING IS NOT WINNING

"God hasn't retained many of us as lawyers, but He has subpoenaed all of us as witnesses!" (Heart and Life).

Peter Stam stepped into the elevator. For a brief moment he was alone with the lady operator. Moody Monthly tells how he never missed an opportunity to witness for the Lord. This was to be no exception:

"I hope your last trip will be up and not down!"

The girl was startled by his remark. She had an idea what he meant, but she was afraid to respond. So she chuckled instead. That prompted brother Stam to say a little more:

"I'm seventy years old, dear girl. And one of these days I'll be meeting my Savior, Jesus Christ. I hope to meet you there."

Then the elevator door opened and others came into the car. Brother Stam stepped out and was on his way. Someone might ask, "Why didn't he linger to see if the girl could be pressed for a decision?" I don't know. Likely he sensed it was not the right time for a soul-winning interview and was content to be a witness. Sometimes a person has to be content with being a witness rather than a soul-winner. They are not the same, you know.

WITNESSING IS NOT WINNING

Come with me to a courtroom. Here we'll see the difference between soul-winning and witnessing. This is the place to observe the difference between the two specialties. They are very distinct skills, as you will see.

18

Watch now, a witness is being called to testify. He rises from his seat and moves to the witness stand. When he is seated, he is asked to make statements from his own personal knowledge. He tells what he knows. Never does he probe or challenge. He gives forth what is asked of him and that's all. Then he is dismissed. That's the extent of his role.

Now watch the prosecutor. He doesn't take the stand. He's a lawyer. It's not his business to tell what he knows. Instead he is highly skilled in extracting information from others and using their words to prove his point. He's a sharp handler of people. He knows how to take facts and present them to win cases. That's his business. All of his moves are aimed at getting a conviction. He works to get a decision out of a judge or jury.

The soul-winner is like a prosecuting attorney. His moves are calculated to extract information from a prospect. He uses that information, in cooperation with the Holy Spirit, to bring conviction. Then he maneuvers his prospect to the point where he must face Christ. Far from telling a person what he knows, his efforts are all geared to getting a prospect to DO SOMETHING about Jesus. He's not content to tell people anything. He wants them to ACT, to do something about the Savior standing at the door of their hearts.

● When we see the difference between a prosecuting attorney and a witness, we are in a position to note the difference between a soul-winner and a witness. They are two different specialties. As long as a man simply tells another ABOUT Jesus, he is a witness. But the moment he tries to get that person to DO SOMETHING with Christ, he shifts over to the role of the soul-winner.

Soul-winning consists of a single task—bringing a prospect face to face with Christ and pressing him to receive the Lord as his Savior. There's no half-way business about it. You either get a man to make his decision or you don't. If you fail to make the presentation or are interrupted for some reason, you simply do not win that soul. If there is no decision, there is no soul-winning. Witnessing on the other hand, is a work which can be performed in countless ways. The moment a person does **anything** to share the word of Christ, he is a 100% success. Witnessing ranges all the way from hiding a gospel tract in a public place to telling another what Jesus means to you.

Thus—soul-winning and witnessing are NOT the same. While everyone can witness for Jesus, not everyone can win souls—at least not at first.

THAT'S IMPORTANT TO KNOW

I was in an evangelical church bringing a series on witnessing. At the end of the first lecture a tearful lady hurried forward to speak to me. She was nervous and perspiring. Her hands kept tearing at a knotted handkerchief:

"Dr. Lovett, I'm ashamed to say this, but I just can't witness for the Lord. I don't know how to win souls. I've never had any kind of training and I'm so scared, I'm afraid to try."

"Forget soul-winning," I said to her. "Put it out of your mind. I'm not going to ask you or anyone else in this class to win souls. This is a course on witnessing, not soul-winning."

The moment she heard I wasn't expecting her to win souls, her shoulders dropped in relief. Like many others, she thought she couldn't be a witness for the Lord without being a soul-winner. When I explained the difference between winning and witnessing, joy brightened her face. Her fear of soul-winning had so blinded her mind, she hadn't grasped one of the techniques I demonstrated in the first session.

So I took a moment and gave her some **easy** helps for getting started as a witness. She went away rejoicing. She was ready now to get serious about witnessing. But as long as she thought witnessing meant winning souls, she was too terrified to learn anything. Until that night she didn't realize there was an easy way to get started in the business of reaching others for Jesus.

How many are like that?

For more than two decades I have been training soul-winners and witnesses. It has been my experience that the average Christian doesn't know the difference between the two skills. Most think they are synonymous. That causes them to shy away from any kind of training. Believing there is no way to witness short of winning a soul to Christ, they are reluctant to start. A multitude of God's people is content to remain silent, thinking only those prepared to win souls are qualified to speak for Christ.

I estimate that 80% of all believers have this notion. Satan is using it to keep them out of action. I don't blame them for being frightened. Soul-winning is a terrifying business—

21

until you are equipped with the skill, **and more importantly**, have the STRENGTH to use it. It's a welcome relief, therefore, to learn that there are two specialties—one which is quite difficult and the other very easy. It becomes obvious, then, that many who have shied away from witnessing, thinking it meant soul-winning, could get started.

> **NOTE: Since this book is on witnessing, you will find no soul-winning skill offered in these pages. My approach to that task is set forth in another volume, SOUL-WINNING MADE EASY. It offers the ENCOUNTER-METHOD of winning souls, which is a four-step plan for presenting Christ alive. It shows how to maneuver a person to the place where he beholds Jesus standing at the door of his heart. It gives you the very words to use in leading a person to receive Christ. It's a very sharp skill and extremely successful. However, I recommend that the average reader develop skill as a witness before attempting to win souls.**

FORGET SOUL-WINNING?

 Does it sound as if I am saying to you, "Don't win souls?" You could get that idea. What I am really saying is, "Witness first and then win souls." It's a wonderful thing to bring people face to face with Jesus and then watch the Lord save them right before your eyes. I thrill to that delicious work myself. I wish that every Christian could know the heart-pounding delight that goes with it. Honestly, I don't think there is anything in Christian work to match it.

I believe that all Christians COULD become soul-winners—IF they would first work with the Holy Spirit as witnesses. There is nothing more torturous than forcing yourself to be a soul-winner when you don't have the personality strength for that kind of work. The thing to do is to develop your strength as a witness, and then you can tackle the task of soul-winning with confidence and enthusiasm. I am suggesting, that unless you have a vigorous personality strength which allows you to start right off as a soul-winner, you should forget about it— **for a while.**

● Now there are some people, who, by virtue of their personality gifts, can start immediately as soul-winners. Usually these are salesmen or those who hold public jobs. They are psychologically equipped as social aggressives. They find it easy to manipulate other people. A Christian with such personality traits we could call a natural born soul-winner. All he needs is to be equipped with a plan, and he could start winning souls—**instantly.** But let me assure you, people like that are a MINORITY. The average Christian does NOT have that kind of social strength. Therefore, it is wrong, very wrong, to suppose a shy and timid believer ought to pattern himself after one who is naturally forceful with other people.

> **OBSERVE:** "Doesn't the Spirit's power make up for deficiencies in our personalities?" Is that what you're asking? The answer is, yes. But He doesn't do it AUTO-MATICALLY. We must learn to work with Him at close range before His strength becomes our strength. That kind of know-how doesn't come overnight. It's one thing to say God's Spirit does this and that for us, it's quite another to experience that working in an actual situation. The average Christian wouldn't recognize the working of the Holy Spirit in a live situation, knowing only the theory of His ministry. It takes time and experimentation to become familiar with the Spirit's power. That's why I urge all believers to witness first and then win souls.

EVERY CHRISTIAN SHOULD WITNESS

The Lord is aware of this variable in His people. He knows some are endowed with public gifts, while others are shy and timid. That's why He gave the command to witness. . ."Ye shall be My witnesses" (Acts 1:8). Everyone can witness, even though not all go on to win souls. Why? There are ways to witness that match the shyness of the most timid soul. Take the little old lady who won't even sing loudly in church.

Could she boldly approach someone for Christ? Never in a 1000 years. Yet she could enclose a tract in a letter or card to a friend. And how about the factory worker who trembles as he goes by the front office. Can he be expected to move in on people with the claims of Christ? Hardly. Yet he could toss a tract in a car in the parking lot.

The Lord Jesus installed the witnessing program to accomodate this variable in His people. Everyone can begin with the easiest steps, and then, with the passing of time, graduate to harder ones. It is cruel to expect people to perform spiritual tasks that are not consistent with their social strengths. No it's worse than that, it's hazardous. There are those who accept the challenge of their pastor or some evangelist to try and be soul-winners. A sense of duty drives them. For a time they go through the nightmare of attempting something beyond their ability, but it doesn't last. Before long, they recoil from it. And that's bad. Usually it instills a fear from which they are not easily recovered.

> NOTE: Christians can be reminded of their obligation to Jesus and then be browbeaten into soul-winning, but it's a cruel thing to do to them. There is no joy in slavish conformity to the Great Commission. More than one has been rushed into soul-winning, only to give it up later when it proved to be a joyless duty. It's risky business to turn people sour on reaching others for Christ. Far better is it to start them off as witnesses, and let their strengths accumulate. Then, as they acquire first hand experience of what the Holy Spirit can do through them, there's a good chance they will go on and become soul-winners. Does not even God refuse to tempt us beyond that which we are able (1 Cor. 10:13). Why should we overly stress those who are not ready to be rushed into soul-winning?

SHOULD EVERY CHRISTIAN LEARN TO WIN SOULS?

Yes, and that is not a contradiction of what I have just said. I have simply stated that most Christians should **start off** as witnesses rather than soul-winners. But that doesn't mean they should forget soul-winning completely. I would hope for the opposite. If a man will take witnessing seriously, he has a fine chance of building his strengths to the place where he can become an effective soul-winner.

But the question I asked was "Should every Christian LEARN to win souls?" The emphasized word is learn. There's a difference between learning a soul-winning plan and using it. Even if a person feels he could never lead a soul to Christ, he should acquire the mechanics for doing it anyway. Why?

There's a screech of tires, then the sickening thud of crumpling metal and the tinkle of broken glass. You look up from your paper. Was that an auto accident? Shortly there comes the sound of excited voices. You go to the front door and look outside. Why there was an accident, right in front of your house.

You rush outside to see what you can do. There's a body spilled out on the street. Is the person alive? You move in for a closer look. Yes, he's alive. His eyes flutter. You look down at him. His lips move. You bend over to hear. His hand grabs your leg:

"Help me, please. I'm not a Christian. I don't want to die like this. Tell me how to be saved!"

See what I mean? Everyone who has received Christ should equip himself for that moment when ANYONE could lead a soul to Jesus—if he knew how. You never know when a neighbor might have such a burden he is compelled to come to you for relief. Suppose he clumsily says, "I feel the need of God in my life. Can you help me?" Wouldn't it be awful to be unprepared in that moment? Why, the shiest Christian alive could lead that person to Jesus—if he knew how.

So—every Christian should EQUIP himself with some method for presenting Christ, even if he never plans to use it. There's no guarantee that someday, someone will not say to you, **"What must I do to be saved?"**

What of the bolder person?

That Christian who moves easily among people, or has little difficulty engaging others in conversation, should learn to win souls. If he doesn't, he will have to account for his failure at the judgment seat of Christ. It is impossible for any of us to dodge our responsibility under the Great Commission. But now I'm going to surprise you. Even though a man has the strength to win souls, he should **also** take a systematic course in witnessing. You didn't expect that, did you? You'd think someone who was already winning souls, wouldn't need to bother with witnessing skills. Right?

There are so many wondrous insights to be gained through witnessing. A person picks up all sorts of techniques for working with the Holy Spirit in the most intimate situations. These precious strengths pay off beautifully when one finally graduates into soul-winning. But those Christians who go DIRECTLY into soul-winning often lack the poise and relaxation a witnessing course would have given them. Some work hard for each decision, having not yet learned how much the Spirit of God is ready to do for them.

> **NOTE:** A soul-winner cannot possibly use his skill on every person crossing his path. Many around him cannot be reached for a soul-winning interview. Therefore, he should be continually working with the various witnessing techniques for the sake of those otherwise inaccessible souls. It would be a shame if his soul-winning skill made him feel responsible only for those he could reach with an interview. No serious minded Christian can eliminate witnessing from his life, even though he might be the most skilled soul-winner to appear on earth.

SEE—YOU'VE BEEN HELPED ALREADY

The confusion is now gone. You have come to understand that soul-winning and witnessing are two separate specialties. This really helps. It allows each Christian to survey his personality gifts and consider which area is best for him. Those with outstanding public gifts and social grace, should get busy learning the soul-winning plan. The sooner they do, the sooner they can have the FUN of closing a deal for Christ.

The rest can look forward to getting started with witnessing exercises that will not over-stress them. It's a relief to know that there are skills which match your shyness and accomodate your timid nature. What God really wants from all of us is—faithfulness. Those who have yet to develop their personality strength, need only to be faithful in learning how to witness. Those equipped with social strengths can be equally faithful by acquiring a soul-winning plan and using it.

Now then, aren't you comforted to learn that the witness is not the prosecutor? That one can be a witness without being a soul-winner? Of course. It has to be this way, since God has made us all differently. So heave a sigh of relief. Believe me when I tell you that witnessing is a separate ministry, one which has its own gentle techniques. If you will, then we have taken. . .

THE FIRST WORRY OUT OF WITNESSING!

As you read the next chapter, there is another worry that will disappear. You could be surprised when you learn what it is.

Chapter Three

ADVENTURE IN POWER!

Some years ago there appeared in "Life" magazine a full page photo taken in the aftermath of a midwestern tornado. I thought the sight incredible. In the center of the picture was a telephone pole with a piece of straw driven through it. But audiences tell me they have seen this very thing. How can anything as weak and helpless as a piece of straw be driven through something as rugged as a telephone pole?

 The answer packs a terrific lesson. That straw, while weak in itself, was surrendered to the tornado. Through this surrender, the power of the tornado **became the power of the straw.** That helpless piece of straw actually moved in the power of the tornado. A shy, weak, and timid Christian can do the same—in the power of God!

Open your mouth in the name of Jesus and the anointing of the Holy Spirit follows. As ridiculous as it might seem, a weak little Christian can move in the power of the Holy Spirit—through surrender! And believe me, it is fun! Here is a new world of adventure. Taste the thrill of God's power, and it will surpass anything this world has to offer. No child of God can claim to have the abundant life without the power of God.

THE EXCITEMENT BUTTON

Some years ago I was entombed a quarter-mile deep in concrete. It was the control room of the great Hoover Dam. You could sense the fantastic pressures exerted against the outside. That deafening roar of those mighty generators added to the awesomeness.

"See that button?" The superintendent was pointing to the control panel. "If I should push it, it would start that third generator over there and supply enough power for the city of Los Angeles."

Wow! Was I impressed. But I was wholly unprepared for his next words.

"Press it!" I couldn't believe my ears.

"I mean it, press it." He did mean it. But it was a nervous finger that stretched out.

I touched the button! And pushed!

The tonnage of Lake Mead struck the blades of the turbine. The concrete trembled. How exciting! I had merely moved a finger and now a three story monster was beginning to whine. The generator was working. I wasn't listening when the superintendent said it was change-over time and that he was to start it up anyway. All I knew was I had pushed and there was power. What a thrill!

I don't suppose very many people have pushed that button in Hoover Dam, but every child of God has access to an even more important button. Did you know there is a button that releases the power of God? That's the real excitement button! Now all of us hear about God's power. Some think about it, others talk about it, and even pray about it. But how many have pushed that Button? Yet, it is within reach. The Superintendent of Heaven says. . ."PUSH IT!" All anyone has to do to have the power of God in his life is **push the button.**

GOD'S BUTTON

Look closely at God's power button and you will find it is clearly marked "GO." Just two little letters and they spell the difference between the power-filled life and a routine one. The power formula is bound up in that one word. Jesus put it this way. . ."Go—and I'll go with you." Are you ready to believe those few words hold the key to power in your life?

Look at the words just ahead of the Great Commission:

"All authority in heaven and earth is given unto Me, go ye. . ."

And what is the next word? If your Bible isn't open you might not know. I ask this of audiences all over the land and they don't know right away. The word is "THEREFORE." And what is the "therefore," there for? Look back. Because all power and authority in heaven has been delegated. Jesus offers the resources of heaven to those who will get involved with Him in the witnessing program.

Who hasn't heard "GO and LO" sermons? Everyone. So the invitation reads, "You go first and I'll go with you." There's the secret of the power-filled life. We move **first** and then discover the Lord is with us. Learn this, and there is nothing in the plan of God you cannot do. Ignore it, and you will remain a routine Christian.

YOU GO FIRST

We live in a day when it is easier to understand the working of God's power. Many things we use daily are power-operated. For example, consider power-steering on a car. You know about power-steering don't you? There is a unit under the hood that is actuated by the engine and supplies the power for turning the wheels. Just imagine a roaring 300 horsepower giant twisting the front wheels of your car. That should be easy for him, right?

But with the huge engine running all that power does nothing to those front wheels until you move the steering wheel in the front seat of the car. The moment you turn that steering wheel, the 300 horsepower giant springs to action and twists the front wheels in either direction. But until that steering wheel is turned, nothing happens. It wouldn't matter if there were 500 or 5000 horsepower available, nothing happens until the steering wheel is turned. That twisting power waits.

See the application? As Christians, we have the Holy Spirit. In fact, "If any man have not the Spirit of Christ, he is none of His!"* So that much is settled. With the power of the Holy Spirit "under the hood," (if you will permit the imagery) we have power—all the power of the Godhead residing within us. That is where the "All authority in heaven and earth" is located.

The principle holds true. With all that indwelling power, nothing happens until we push the "GO" button. We have to move **first**. We have to start. Until we open our mouths for Christ, the power of God just waits and waits and waits!

PROVE IT

One of the comforts of writing such lines is that the statements are provable—**in your own life!** Nothing I have said cannot be demonstrated to your own satisfaction. All you need do is try and see. Don't think to challenge me until you have tried them for yourself.

---

*Rom. 8:9.

When these truths were first becoming operative in my own life, I was eager to test them, just as I suggest you do. There's an incident that strengthens me every time I think of it.

● I had an appointment with a Christian industrialist who was interested in my ministry, and we were to go to lunch. His bookkeeper was invited to go along. My friend thought I might be able to deal with him. But right off the bat, the unsaved man informed me he had been worked on by the best. He avowed it would be a waste of time for me to try to lead him to Christ. From the tone of his voice, I knew he was right.

But the Holy Spirit prompted this thought, "Why not try an experiment with this hard-hearted man?" And then a little scheme presented itself. As we sat at the table, my friend excused himself and left me alone with the prospect. I turned to him:

"You made it clear to me you were not interested in any attempt to introduce you to Christ."

"That's right."

"Would you permit me to make a little experiment, just for my own sake? It really is not for you at all, and I'll not seek to persuade you about anything. It is for my own benefit entirely, but I need your help. All I want to do is say a few sentences to you. . .OK?"

"I guess so. . ." He was suspicious, but curious.

"First, I want to tell you that this world in which we live is no accident. That it is all planned and maintained by God. Even our meeting today is right on schedule. This is because God loves you. He thinks you are precious and would like to have you for His personal friend. And there is no limit to what He would do to make it possible for you to like Him and be with Him forever."

32

He was actually nodding his head, but I doubt if he were aware of it. There is much that goes on inside a person when he listens to God's truth from another. So often it is unnoticed. I continued:

> "Now I'm telling you that He loves you so much that He sent His Son to die for you. A clear demonstration that He is head over heels in love with you. Right now He is waiting to forgive every sin in your life, share His own life with you and offer you all that He has. Even now He will come into your heart and reveal Himself to you, if you would just give Him a chance."

I was looking him squarely in the eye as I spoke this. Everything was important now, for this was an experiment. I really didn't care what the man said at this moment, I was watching to see how the Holy Spirit would perform His ministry. What would He do? I pressed my point.

"DO YOU BELIEVE THAT?"

He hesitated a moment. I thought. . .but then. . .he slowly shook his head.

"NO!"

But he was lying. In the corner of each eye a tear had formed, and one rolled out onto his cheek. He believed the testimony, all right. In fact, he **knew** it was true. Hence the tears. But in spite of what he knew to be true, he didn't want anything to do with Christ. Okay, that was his own business. He would answer to God for that.

What a lesson! The Holy Spirit had done His work. Faithfully, He bore witness to my words. He let me see that tear roll out giving an external witness of His working. How I thanked Him for that tear! My heart leaped for joy. I knew the Holy Spirit was using me now, no matter what words to the contrary came from the prospect's mouth. What a thrilling discovery.

I pass it on to you. I guarantee that the Spirit of God will bear witness to your words as readily as He will to mine. You can discount much of what people say back, when you witness. In spite of any balkiness on the part of a prospect, you can know God is faithfully talking to his heart **as you speak.** Once you try this, the Spirit will grant you plenty of evidence. He has no favorites. He will do for you just what He has done for me.

● Prove Him. Turn on your light and let Him demonstrate a mighty power that seemingly comes right out of you. Put Him to the test and learn by experience He will back your witness all the way. Once you learn that your words are **always** followed by the Holy Spirit's power, you. . .

TAKE THE SECOND WORRY OUT OF WITNESSING!

THE ROUTINE CHRISTIAN

Those who will not open their mouths for Christ publicly, cannot have the power of God! And without the power of God, they must content themselves with a routine existence. They can never be as rich as the one who witnesses. Oh, they may claim a wealth of stored-up Bible teachings and memorized Scripture verses. But they are a long way from the abundant life Jesus offers those who **obey.**

Now it is true that there are treasures in God's Word, and they help in the midst of trial, but I submit that moving in the power of God is the greatest treasure of all. There simply can be no abundant life without the power of God. It is the proper inheritance of every child of God and one who does not enjoy this experience is living on a lower plane. It is not possible to have the real fulness of God in your life without being a witness.

"And ye shall be witnesses unto me. . ." (Acts 1:8).

What a waste. All that indwelling power for witnessing and Christians not living in it. It hurts me to think of the waste within modern Christianity when the host of God is silent for Jesus. Was it not for this very reason that our Lord terminated His fleshly ministry? Did He not wish to indwell us in the Spirit that we might have the privilege of doing His work in POWER!

"Greater works than these shall ye do because I go to my Father. . ." (John 14:12).

Who could dream that any of God's people would toss away such a wonderful inheritance. I'll bet the angels are shocked!

Let a man begin to speak out for Jesus (outside the church) and he enters a wonderland where all things are changed by the power of God. It is a new kind of excitement. He may find an astonishing wisdom on his lips, or see doors fling open that others said could never be opened. He will find himself doing things for Jesus he thought he could never do. He will see hard-hearted and rugged people weep before his words. He will find himself in the midst of amazing witnessing situations. Doors open everywhere. A new glory fills his soul. He may even cry for God to shut off the blessing for fear of dying with joy. But even so he has entered the abundant life!

● Margie and I sat with some dear friends at the Los Angeles Billy Graham Crusade in 1963 and it was an amazing spectacle to watch thousands pour forth from the stands in response to Billy's invitation. There was power there, no doubt about that. His mouth was open. But when my friends turned and said, "Isn't that the most wonderful sight!" the Holy Spirit struck me with this challenge and it became my answer:

"Yes, but there is an even more glorious one."

"Oh. . .What?"

35

"Reaching souls with a witness from your own lips."

And it's true. I thrilled to see the crowds go forward at the Coliseum. But I have had the greater thrill of seeing people penetrated for Christ as a result of God's anointing of my own lips. That is what the Lord offers **each** Christian.

WILLING?

Can you picture yourself going about in the power of God? You might jar a few lives if you do. How does the prospect of seeing your power-words upsetting others strike you? Maybe you don't want to be a disturber for Jesus? But is there any choice? If you are going to witness, there will be power! That power means conviction for somebody. If you are faithful to open your mouth, people are going to be convicted by the Holy Spirit, that's all there is to it.

"But maybe someone will think I'm a crackpot if I go around with this effect on others?"

Likely some will. Just as they regarded your Savior and the apostles as crackpots. But you will be in distinguished company. You won't really mind once you taste the thrill of the Holy Spirit. Seeing Him use you will overshadow much of what others may think. That is where boldness comes from, you know—the Holy Spirit. Your courage will have deep roots in Him once you experience that first time He backs your mention of Jesus. He has a precious device for sweeping away fears in the course of an actual witness. But I'm saving that for later.

 Learn then, the sweet science of working with the Holy Spirit. Gain the skill of moving in His power and your witnessing will acquire an attractiveness that will eliminate most of the "crackpotness" from your work. It is possible to become so skillfull in witnessing and working with the Holy Spirit, that you acquire a

winsomeness. I believe this is the kind most effective in our land today. We live among a sophisticated and knowledgeable people, and we are the most powerful for Christ when we display the fewest thorns.

Master the principles of this book and you will be that kind of a witness. You will have the time of your life in the power of God and live on the highest spiritual plane. Learning what to do and say in the power of the Spirit can,

TAKE THE THIRD WORRY OUT OF WITNESSING!

Here's how we cast out worry. . .

1. When we learn that witnessing does not mean soul-winning, we get rid of the first worry.

2. When we learn that the Spirit's power follows our words, we get rid of the second worry.

3. When we learn exactly what to do and say, we get rid of the third worry.

The remaining chapters tell **HOW.** There's an easy way to start. Next.

Chapter Four

YOUR PRIVATE WORLD

The preacher has just finished a terrific message on the Great Commission. With stirring words he set forth the Christian's responsibility to reach others for Christ. You shake his hand afterwards, encouraging him with the usual words, "That was just great, pastor, I wish every Christian could have heard that today." Then you pass through the front doors into the bright sunlight. Yes sir, it is good to be stirred by God's Word.

The challenge still rings in your heart, "Go ye into all the world. . ."

As you move down the sidewalk to your car, the Holy Spirit prods your mind with a question, "How can I go into all the world?" The answer comes quickly, "There's no way for one man to reach the whole world." You're right. Nothing could be more obvious. How then does the Great Commission apply to you? Surely it sends you someplace, but where? If you cannot reach the entire world, what world can you reach? There is only ONE world any man can reach. . .his own PRIVATE world.

PRIVATE WORLD?

Indeed. Everyone has a private world. It consists of his weekly routine.

The center of man's private world is his home. From there he ranges to his job, does errands, finds pleasure, and goes to church. No matter where he goes or what he does, his **home is the hub.** That's where he sleeps and eats. He always comes back at the end of the day. In the course of daily living, he has a routine, a pattern he follows most of the time. For the average Christian, it consists of job, shopping, church, and recreation.

Within the Christian's private world are those whose paths cross his as he goes about the daily cycle of three meals, on the job, and back to bed. In the course of that routine, he rubs shoulders with people he can influence for Christ better than anyone else. Why? They are inside his private world. Think of all the souls in and around you as you go about your routine of living. Wouldn't you say a multitude circulates in your private world? Visually it might look like this:

YOUR PRIVATE WORLD

PHONE BOOTH
GAS STATION
LIBRARY

MARKET

JOB

LAUNDROMAT
CAR WASH
CLEANERS

CHURCH

HOME
CENTER OF
SPIRITUAL LIFE

SOCIAL
EVENTS

RESTAURANT

STORES
BARBER
SCHOOL
DOCTOR'S OFFICE

RECREATION

BANK
NEIGHBORS
POST OFFICE
BEAUTY PARLOR

As you move in your world, there are people you **contact more** than anyone else. There are individuals who **mean more** to you than anyone else. And there are those whom you **influence more** than anyone else. In some cases you may be the only concerned Christian **in touch** with them. To these souls, you are God's man more clearly than Billy Graham. You can reach them. He can't. He doesn't have your relationship with them.

When Jesus said, "Go ye into all the world and preach the gospel," did He mean for us to go running off someplace, like India or Africa? Hardly. We'd end up playing musical countries. And after we got to these countries, what would we do? We could still reach no more souls than those found in our private world. Once on the field we would again be limited to those we contacted as we moved out from our home base and returned.

● Clearly our Lord's command was NOT an order to travel, but to start reaching those around us. When He said, "Ye shall be My witnesses," He had in mind our reaching the lost within our private worlds. The command to GO sends each of us into the multitude found within the circle of our weekly routine. It is the ONLY world anyone can reach. Therefore, I ask, if you don't reach your own private world. . .

WHO WILL?

AROUND THE WORLD

I mean the circle of your private world. You go a number of places out of necessity. What Christian doesn't work or shop or make trips to the bank and post office? Do you drive a car? Then you make stops at gas stations. The person who waits on you is a prospect in your private world.

You eat, of course. That takes you to the market for food. Clerks assist you. Cashiers take your money. Box boys help with the sacks, often escorting you to your car. As you walk alongside that young man, you represent the Lord Jesus. He cares about that boy. He died for him. What do you think the Lord would have you do about it?

The next time you are in the bank or post office, take a look at the people making out deposit slips and examining their mail. They stop at those tables, perhaps hundreds in a day. Those tables are terrific outposts for Christ. They are directly in the path of your private world. You could use them to reach lost souls subtly and easily, if you knew how. Then there are drug stores, beauty shops, discount houses, libraries, phone booths, variety stores, laundromats, and repair shops, to name but a few. Each time you enter such a place, you intersect a "people-path" within your private world.

If you eat out now and then, a waitress serves you. Likely she gets close enough to touch. There you sit with the greatest news man has ever heard. Please don't tell me you are immune to her need of Christ. She's another prospect in your private world.

How many trips will a man make to gas stations during the rest of his life? Thousands, wouldn't you say? How many times will he go to lunch? Again, thousands. What will be the total of his trips to the shops and stores in the years ahead? How many souls will he brush on the job, see on vacation trips, speak to at amusement centers, or on recreational outings? More thousands, of course. See what I mean? There are masses of people inside your private world waiting for the invitation to Christ.

• Weigh this: if a man leaves Christ out of all that, what place does Jesus have in his life? The weekly routine is the sum of one's life on earth. If a Christian is not interested in reaching his private world for Christ, can he honestly say he has made Jesus Lord of his life? Hardly. The opposite is true. He has excluded Jesus from the bulk of his life.

I know that sounds harsh, but we might as well face it right here. If Christ is excluded from the believer's daily

41

routine, what's left for Him? A few hours of church each week. That's all Jesus gets. Oh there may be a tithing of money and some extra meetings thrown in, but such a Christian lives pretty well for himself—not Christ. He shuns the Lord's clearest command and goes about his business living for himself. Obviously he cares nothing about lost souls, even worse, he cares nothing about obeying Christ as his Master. Every Christian is saved to serve Jesus. That is an inescapable fact (2 Cor. 5:15).

DO YOU CARE?

A host of people in your private world can be reached almost effortlessly—**if you care enough to bother.** I mean care enough about Jesus. I can see how one might not be too concerned about lost souls, especially those he never sees. But surely every believer ought to care about Christ. Jesus died for us. We owe Him all we are and have. Isn't it enough that He asks us to reach these people with His invitation? The Christian who won't even bother (the more so when a plan like this falls into his hands) should ask himself if he really loves the Lord.

Now consider the man who does love Jesus and accepts the commission to reach his private world. No longer does he go to the store just to buy THINGS. He is aware that he belongs to Jesus, that many lost souls are in the market place. Instead of, "Now what was it my wife wanted me to get?" he asks himself, "How will I serve the Lord on this trip?" No longer does he stop at the gas station just to buy gas. Now it's, "What does Jesus want me to do for Him now that He has brought me to this station?" Even when he goes to the restaurant, his mind is not limited to his stomach or a good time with friends. "I've got to make this outing count for Christ," he says, "He is my Master every moment of my time."

That's the way you will feel about Jesus' ownership of your life, when the truth of your private world burns in your imagination. There is no way to give your best to Jesus and leave Him out of your private world. When it strikes a Christian that he has been wasting most of his life by settling down in the world rather than reaching it for Christ, he is humbled by the realization. To find that he has been substituting church-going for personal obedience to the Great Commission, is a Damascus Road experience. The dramatic effect it can have on one's life is equal to the turnabout of the apostle Paul. A fantastic thing occurs in the believer when he is seized by the thought that he is commissioned to reach his private world.

BUT THE DEVIL TWISTS THE COMMAND

Satan hates the truth of the Christian's private world. He'll do all he can to keep believers from learning of it. That's why you seldom, if ever, hear it mentioned. He'd rather have Christians think of the "world" as some distant place where a missionary goes. Every time a missionary is commissioned the devil whispers, "See, that man is off to obey the Great Commission." But it is a lie. As soon as the missionary arrives at his new station, what will he do? He will start reaching his own private world. That's ALL he can do.

NOTE: A foreign missionary simply changes home base. Once on the field he can only reach those found within his daily routine. That's all anyone can do no matter WHERE he lives. Geography has nothing to do with the Great Commission. Does not the missionary live in a house? Does he not eat three meals a day? From his home base he ranges forth to perform the tasks required by his way of life—the same as anyone else. His contacts are still limited to those souls found INSIDE his daily routine. True he has received a call to CHANGE LOCATIONS, but that has nothing to do with the commission. He (like ourselves) is obligated to obey Christ's command no matter where he lives. Every Christian is called as a missionary to his own private world.

Satan also deceives Christians with respect to supporting a pastor. Since they pay his salary, they feel they are sharing in his witnessing, soul-winning, baptizing, etc. And they are—**as an investment.** But helping him obey HIS call cannot be substituted for obeying their own call. While they are helping him reach his private world, what are they doing about their own? It remains neglected. That's the one they've been called to reach. There is absolutely no way for a Christian to HIRE a substitute. Investing in someone else's ministry is no substitute for fulfilling your own. There is no substitute for personal obedience.

> **OBSERVE: Imagine you have engaged a retired minister to be at your side 24 hours a day. You have hired him to do all of your witnessing for you. He accompanies you wherever you go, contacting as many as possible within your private world. That's what it would take, you see, if we're even to approach the idea of hiring a substitute. But then who actually obeys the Lord? Who finally gets the reward for obedience? When you stand before the Judge in the last day, will your substitute be there? All the money in the world couldn't get a sober Christian to be your substitute in that day. When God asks for the record of your personal obedience to the Great Commission, you will be on your own.**

BUT IT'S SCAREY OUT THERE

The moment you start thinking of your private world as a mission field, it's not so friendly any more. When you go about minding your own business (not Christ's), there's nothing to fear. You could shop the stores, eat in the restaurants, buy gas for your car, all without a particle of threat. You can feel comfortable and quite at ease. After all, the surroundings are familiar, and there's no reason for anyone to be upset with you. As long as you do not attempt to serve Christ in your private world, you can remain very much at home.

44

The Christian's private world is an unfriendly place. With the exception of his residence and his church, it is enemy territory. It belongs to the devil (2 Cor. 4:4; 1st Jo. 5:19). It is a hostile place. Outspoken Christians are not welcome. Those who witness openly are not popular. The world doesn't like them. But neither does it like their Lord, and He made the world (Col. 1:16). Can His servants expect to be treated any better if they identify themselves with Him? Jesus warned they wouldn't.

The Christian has to decide which it will be: friendship with the world (which means keeping silent about Christ), or friendship with God (which means obeying His orders). The believer can't have it both ways. God's Word is very blunt about that:

"Friendship with the world is enmity with God" (Ja. 4:4).

Fear of man has silenced most of God's people. Yet, inside their churches they are not so secretive. Often they are quite loud in declaring their love for Christ. Yet, in the world and on their jobs, their union with Christ is a well kept secret. It's so easy to be bold for the Lord inside the protective walls of a church building. It's easy to shout His praises amidst the approving smiles of agreeing brethren. It's so easy to appear aggressive for Him when it is all talk. But what happens to those same Christians once they go outside those four walls?

It's a different story then. The boldness fades, the shouts are stifled, and the singing turns to silence. It takes a great deal of courage to speak out for the Lord when one is on his own, out there in his private world. It's a lot easier to invite people to come inside a church building than it is to take the gospel to them in enemy territory. There are very few today who will do anything for Christ—outside the church. Yet, that's where the Great Commission takes us. We were not told, "Go ye into all the church."

HERE'S WHAT I MEAN

 When I was researching the truth that people scare people, I visited many churches. On one occasion I was visiting a particular church, watching the people carefully. During testimony time an old saint rose to his feet. The pastor, who sat next to me, nudged—"He's going to quote Philippians 4:13, wait and see." Apparently this was the old man's favorite verse. It seemed that everyone else also knew what he was going to say.

"I can do all things through Christ which strengthenth me!"

There was such vigor in his voice. You could feel the fever in his words. He was loud and full of sincerity. I was interested in this man. I liked his gusto, his unashamed declaration for Christ. He stood tall in my eyes. The pastor further told me he was one of the most faithful, outspoken members of his congregation.

When the service ended I followed him out the front door. He was so soldierly for Jesus inside the church, I wondered what he would be like **outside.** He walked down the front steps. He had gone about 20 feet from the door when a pedestrian stopped him. He was inquiring the way to a certain street. I LISTENED. This was a perfect witnessing opportunity. A child could exploit this for Christ, if he knew how.

Well the man got his **local** directions. That was all. This saint, so aflame moments before, spoke not a word about the true directions, the way to heaven. He could have at least said, "Here are some directions that are even more important to you," and offered a tract. But he didn't even do that.

Now this man was definitely satisfied he could do "all things through Christ." He even told his church he could. Yet, here he was unable to DO ANYTHING for Christ when the opportunity hit him in the face, seconds later. I had to find out about this. When I questioned him, he begged off saying he wasn't called to be a witness. But you and I know that is just an excuse. We can't let anyone get away with that. So I pressed the point, using God's Word with some authority. Finally the truth came out. . .

"I WAS AFRAID!"

This dear soul was reluctant to make this confession, but at last he did. One moment he was boasting of his great power through the indwelling Lord, the next moment he was powerless. He couldn't even do the simplest task. What was wrong? Didn't he care about Jesus? Of course. His heart was full of praise to His precious Savior. For 50 years (that's how long he had been going to church) he had been absorbing the THEORY of Christianity. Yet never once had he set about to develop any ACTION strength. He had made no effort to equip himself for service **outside the church.** In fact, he didn't even know there was another kind of strength to be developed.

So we talked about it.

When he faced the matter squarely, he was baffled by his own feebleness. He couldn't explain why he was so weak and helpless in the face of an **easy** witnessing opportunity. He had been a Sunday school teacher for years. Now he was president of the board of deacons. Those 50 years of soaking in sermons didn't give him an ounce of strength—outside the church. I had no trouble convincing him of the difference between the LECTURE world of the church and the ACTION world of witnessing. When I assured him the strengths he needed for reaching his private world could not be gained in church, he believed me. He, himself, was living proof.

There's only one place a Christian can develop witnessing strengths and that is in the world itself.

A HUNDRED YEARS WOULDN'T HELP

Had that old saint continued in his church for another 50 years, it still wouldn't have given him a speck of witnessing muscle. The **faith-life** is enhanced by going to church, but the action-life is something else. There is no way for a person to acquire ACTION-STRENGTH by soaking in the theory of Christianity. A 100 years of lectures, lessons, sermons, and studies wouldn't add an ounce of witnessing strength to a Christian. Come with me to a gymnasium, and we'll see the difference between theory and action.

The instructor issues orders. He asks his students to place their chairs in a semi-circle before him. There—all are seated where they can see him. He is going to talk about body-building. He has a chart. He points to it as he talks. He describes muscle structure and what it takes to reach the various parts of the body.

As he talks, you feel your waist line begin to shrink. More talking and your shoulders harden. Hours go by and your arm muscles begin to bulge. He talks on. Muscles ripple under your clothes. Your proportions are changing. More hours pass and you have a new figure. By nightfall you possess a fully developed physique in the peak of condition. And all you had to do was sit in your chair and listen to the instructor.

"That's ridiculous," you say? Sure it is. You don't build body muscle by listening to lectures. One has to go through a series of workouts before any changes appear. It takes a lot of sweat and faithful exercising before there is any noticeable improvement. It is equally ridiculous to think witnessing strengths can be acquired by listening to lectures. Just as the athlete must perform physical exercises to develop his body, so must the Christian undertake witnessing exercises to develop himself as a witness. **Faith strengths** are increased in church, but it takes **witnessing-strength** to minister to your own private world. The theory world of church and the action world of witnessing are two different theaters of operation. Christianity is a **lecture-life**, but it is also an **action-life**. For some Christians it is like discovering a new world to learn of the action-life.

YOUR PRIVATE WORLD—a new world?

Had you heard of your private world before? Did you know you were under orders to reach it for Christ? That can be a startling discovery. Perhaps you are meeting it for the first time as you read this book.

The average Christian is content to settle down in the world. He sells himself on the idea that he is spiritual because he goes to church and longs for Jesus' return. So he makes himself at home in the world. While he waits for the Lord, he engages in the struggle to get ahead and be somebody. It never occurs to him that he is the bloodbought servant of Jesus, that his life is no longer his own to live as he pleases. He has one vital job for Christ—reaching his own private world. Sadly, the average Christian doesn't even know about this world. No one seems willing to tell him about it. When he finally does learn of it, it is a shocking discovery.

NOTE: From the moment a Christian awakens in the morning until he puts his head on his pillow at night, he is the Lord's servant, commissioned to reach his private world with Jesus' invitation. Every errand becomes a missionary foray into enemy territory. Every contact with people offers another chance to tell of his Master. He is constantly challenged to find new ways for getting the gospel into the hands of those crossing his path. The 100% Christian

harnesses his routine to getting out the good news. He ceases to live for himself and devotes himself to making Christ known within his private world. For a fuller explanation of the way the 100% Christian operates, read the author's book, THE 100% CHRISTIAN. It will change your life.

The truth of the Christian's private world is all but lost today. We must recover it. If your life is going to count for Christ, this truth must become a part of your working knowledge. That's why I have devoted an entire chapter to it. No longer can your private world remain simply as a place to live, work, and do your shopping. It is a mission field and you are the ONLY missionary who can serve it. That's a frightening thought, but it's true. It could make you gulp.

Now don't feel alone in this. Almost every Christian who meets the truth of his private world for the first time, feels as you do. It's like starting the Christian life all over again. Why? Because we are all beginners when it comes to going into action for Christ—**outside the church.** It's a new ball game. For generations church programs have been geared to getting people INSIDE buildings to hear the gospel. But that era is passing. We are entering the great apostasy predicted for the end time. Instead of huge harvests, we are coming to a time of gleaning. Those who come to Christ in these last days are more apt to be gleaned here and there in the private worlds of individual Christians.

Reaching his private world is a new way of life for the average Christian. Therefore, he has to start at the bottom and work his way up. He will feel like a toddler when he starts. And he will develop as he does the actions. It doesn't matter whether one is a Bible saturated conservative or a "turned on" pentecostal, all are in the same boat. Everyone is a beginner when it comes to reaching his private world in the power of the Holy Spirit. It is a new way of life for almost every believer in America today.

NOTE: In this book I will not dwell much on the DIFFER-
ENCE between the PRESENCE of the Holy Spirit and His
POWER. There is a big difference, to be sure. Many believers
enjoy the Spirit's PRESENCE in church meetings and
devotional times, but God's power is limited to OBEDI-
ENCE. The presence of the Spirit has to do with PRAYER.
The power of the Spirit has to do with the effect of our
words on OTHERS. God's presence can be enjoyed privately,
but His power cannot be seen apart from ministering to
others in Jesus' name. If anyone tells you he has the power
of the Holy Spirit in his life, check and see how he is
reaching his private world. If he isn't, well. . .? Very likely
he is mistaking some evidence of God's presence in his life
for power. Remember: power has to do with RESULTS,
the effect of our words on others. The apostle Paul
cautioned us about this very thing (1 Cor. 4:19,20).

If you are meeting the truth of your private world for the
first time, I sympathize with the shock you feel. Perplexing
questions will surface in your mind. "Where do I begin?
How does a person get started reaching his private world?
What do you do first, whom do you reach first?" I know you
have a lot of questions like that. They will be answered before
long. When you have finished this book, you will know
exactly what to do and HOW. I want you to know this, it is
a lot easier than you think. In fact, my next counsel to you
is going to be, "Take it easy." That's the title of chapter
five.

Chapter Five

TAKE IT EASY

Early this year I was conducting a seminar for a regional conference of churches. A brilliantly educated man constantly took exception to the techniques for handling people in the power of God. He quoted verses to show things could only be done a certain way. It was obvious I had stepped on his theological toes, and you know what that does to people. He was so definite in speaking, one might have taken him for an authority.

I let a few remarks pass between us until it appeared the audience might get involved, then ended it. At the noon-break, I invited him to go to lunch with me. We sat at the table, and he continued to pour out his theories for reaching people. As we were finishing, I spied a waitress in an adjoining room, readying a table for a banquet. She didn't look too busy, and it presented a fine test-situation:

"You seem to have this pretty well settled in your mind, Brother K..."

"I should," He replied. "I've been studying this for years."

Then the bombshell. **"How about letting me see you put your theories to work on that waitress over there!"**

A look of horror crossed his face. Suddenly it was no longer a matter for discussion. His theories faded before his eyes. He was so full of boldness in presenting his ideas to me, but putting them into operation was another matter.

"I. . .I don't, I. . .uh. . ." And then he backed off completely. "I don't think this is the best time."

He was no longer the arrogant challenger. He was scared and showed it. He was meeting head-on the difference between theory and experience, and the abruptness of it floored him.

However, it was fruitful for now he was ready to learn:

"Would you like to be able to talk to that waitress and do it without fear or embarrassment?"

"Well. . .I. . .Yes, I suppose I would." He was meeker now.

I gave him three lines of dialogue and asked him to put them on a piece of paper. As soon as he did this, I gave him a tract to present. The lines were simple:

1. "Pardon me, but do you know of a good church around here?" (Response didn't matter)

2. "Do you go yourself?" (Response does not matter)

3. "It's pretty important to find the right church, wouldn't you say? Even religion can be dangerous. This little folder tells why. I'm sure the Lord would have you read it."

He took those words and walked toward the girl. He trembled some, but he knew I was watching. As scared as he was, he opened his mouth to speak the first line and almost the same instant, a smile crossed his face. Within seconds he was speaking in a convincing style. He returned to our table beaming like a kid when school is out:

"I did it! And you know what?"

"What?" You could sense the excitement.

"It worked like magic. She didn't have any church and when I said the Lord wanted her to read this, she told me, 'You know, I've been wanting to talk to someone. I know I should be going to church or something. Could you come back around 5 o'clock and talk to me?' Brother Lovett, do you have any more of those tracts?"

He was in the clouds. Later I learned it was the very first time he had approached a total stranger to create a witnessing situation. On our way back to the convention hall, I saw him stop and talk with a man selecting a newspaper from the rack outside the restaurant. Then he took a tract from his pocket. I couldn't hear the words, but saw them shake hands and read the big grin on my friend's face.

Yes, we're friends now. And you know, he didn't have one word to say during the afternoon sessions. He was too busy taking notes. He had experienced the difference between theory and practice, and now he was hungry for all the know-how he could get. Three simple lines of dialogue opened a whole new life to this man. He had started to **move**, and the Lord kept His promise. Those words actually had power, and he could see it!

BUT THERE IS AN EASIER WAY

My friend started witnessing the hard way. True, it was simple. But it was hard. He met the matter with shock. He was comfortable one moment, hiding behind theories, and the next moment I had said, "Go talk to that waitress." You don't want to become a witness that way. It's too hard on the nerves. Besides there's a much easier way to begin.

 Let me give you a tongue-in-cheek assignment. That is, I don't really mean for you to do this exercise anyplace but in your imagination. Wait until dark. Then go out onto the street in front of your house. Make sure there is no one around. Is there a car parked at the curb, not far away? Good. Now go boldly up to that car and slap it on the fender. Looking it squarely in the headlight, tell it that it needs to be born again.

That's silly, isn't it? But you could do it. If you felt it were vital to Jesus, you would. You see no one is afraid to witness to cars, trees, or telephone poles. They can't reject us or hold bad thoughts about us. They don't scare us. But it would be a different story if I asked you to say that to the unsaved man

54

next door. You'd be scared to death. Don't bother to deny it. The truth is established, **people scare people.**

You can test what I've said as you sit there. Picture yourself approaching that car under the cover of darkness. Easy, isn't it. Now see yourself contacting a stranger with the gospel. There's a difference in feelings, right? That difference is threat—**ego threat.** We have to be realistic about our fear of man. That fear is real, and we have to deal with it. We won't get anywhere unless we do. Therefore, our plan for producing witnesses must develop strengths that are stronger than our fear of man.

 A baseball lands on your roof. Then there's a knock at the door. Some sheepish youngsters want permission to recover the ball. You give your okay. But as they stand there looking up at your roof, they know it is an impossible height for them. There is no way for them to jump up there. So they ask another favor:

"Do you mind if we borrow your ladder?"

The ladder is leaned against your house. One lad scrambles up and retrieves the ball. What those boys couldn't do in ONE JUMP, they easily managed with a ladder. When the distance is broken up into **easy steps,** there's nothing to it. Now that's a vital observation.

To go from the THEORY world of church to the ACTION world of witnessing, is like going from the ground to the roof of your house. The distance is too great to be covered in one jump. The average Christian can't make it without a ladder. It is impossible for most Christians to make a sudden shift from the silent life of church-going to the action life of witnessing. A person can no more become instantly aggressive, than he can leap from the ground to the roof of his house. Therefore, it is urgent that we provide God's people with a ladder—a witnessing ladder.

55

A witnessing ladder?

Exactly. You see there is so much EGO threat involved in presenting Christ to the unsaved, the FEAR of man silences the average Christian. Rejection is the worst blow that can strike our frail egoes. Inasmuch as we represent a REJECTED Christ, the possibility of rejection is present every time we mention Him. Rejection and the Great Commission go hand in hand, for **"If they have persecuted Me, they will also persecute you. The servant is not greater than his Lord"** (John 15:20; Matt. 10:25). It is the fear of what people will think of us that keeps us from witnessing. They threaten us to the extent that they ridicule us or look down on us. We can't stand that. We'd rather be silent than suffer the scorn of others.

Therefore, the gap between silence and faithful witnessing is one of EGO THREAT. And we have to bridge it. It's a distance which cannot be covered in one jump. But if we can break that same distance up into little bite sized steps, then Christians can learn to witness for Jesus as easily as a lad can scoot up a ladder. If we can help Christians learn to ABSORB ego threat, little by little, in time they can witness for Christ without fear.

Apart from some way to handle that awful threat, the average Christian will do NOTHING for Jesus in the world. Oh yes, he'll go to church. There he will shout among the saints and give bold testimonies of God's working in his life. But once he walks out that front door, he becomes as silent as a mummy. So true is this, that born again believers work alongside each other day after day with neither suspecting the other belongs to Christ.

● **If people scare people,** the place to begin witnessing is AWAY from others. Then, in succeeding steps, ease closer and closer. That way the threat is increased bit by bit. When threat comes to us that way, we can absorb it. Finally, when we learn to handle the worst threats, we are able to witness fearlessly. That's what you want, isn't it? Isn't it obvious that when a Christian learns to conquer his fear of others, he will be able to move boldly into his private world for Christ? But without some way to deal with threat in small doses, the average Christian will never make it.

> **NOTE:** Christian courage is not the absence of fear, but the conquest of it in the power of the Holy Spirit. There is no plan anywhere that **CANCELS** fear. The Lord has not provided for the cancellation of any of our problems. He does promise us the ability to overcome them as we learn to operate in His power. This is true of every area of our lives, even more so in the matter of witnessing. There is no shortcut to victory.

● Now you can guess how the witnessing ladder works. The bottom rung is the least threatening type of witness one can make. The next rung is a little harder offering a bit more threat. The third rung offers still more, and so on all the way up the ladder. By increasing the threat a little more with each step, the witness builds his strengths gradually. By the time he reaches the top of the ladder, he will find himself doing things he never dreamed possible—things which were impossible for him at the beginning.

Now what could be simpler? The strength you gain on each rung of the ladder, puts the next step within reach. When the course is completed, you will have moved from that which was the least threatening to that which would have terrified you at the beginning. This book will have done its job when you are able to talk to a perfect stranger about Jesus and do so with ease and confidence. But see how it takes the witnessing ladder to make it possible. You will never reach a challenging height without it.

A SOLID FOUNDATION

Any ladder must rest on something solid. Our witnessing ladder must have sure footing, too. No one wants to start up a ladder until it is secure and steady, does he? There is a

foundation for our witnessing ladder, and that foundation is **YOUR EXPERIENCE WITH CHRIST.** This is where we begin, with your salvation experience. I don't mean whether or not you are saved—but is your own **experience** clear to you? You can't start up the ladder until it is. So we have to talk about it.

Being in the business of teaching soul-winners and witnesses, brings me into contact with thousands of Christians all over the land. You would be shocked to know how many in our churches have been saved for years and still cannot share with someone else the most elementary facts of the salvation encounter. I have asked lots of old timers in the faith. . .

"What right do you have to call yourself a Christian? Where is your authority for it? And how do you know you really are saved?"

You wouldn't believe the vague and shadowy answers I get from people who claim to be saved for the past 50 years! You can test this for yourself. If you do, get ready for a shock. It may appear a simple thing to put the salvation experience into words, but most of God's people just can't do it. Yet, isn't that the real foundation? Does not our whole Christian life rest on our experience with Jesus? You know it does.

So you see, I can't just ask you to be sure of your experience in Christ. I have to ask you to put it into words—and on paper. Now the character of this book changes. If you don't want to mature in Christ and go on to be a witness for Him. . . **do not read another line.** But if you do, then prepare yourself for **action.** Get ready to **do** something. From now on, forget that I am the author and think of me as your personal friend. I want to help you, and I am going to give you things to DO! Start thinking of me as your coach, and you will have a lot of fun with the steps ahead.

Ready for an assignment? Fine. Here's what I want you to do.

ACTION

Go to the place where you write your letters and take out a pen and some paper. Using the sample letter in the back of the book as a guide, write to me and tell me how you know you are saved. Say to yourself, "What right do I have to call myself a **'born again'** Christian?" Then go on to describe the mechanics of your surety in Christ. Put it into an envelope and send it to me here at Personal Christianity.

 Don't dismiss this as something too simple to bother with. It isn't at all simple. In fact, you will find it is very hard to put thoughts on paper. This is why so many never write to their friends. It is hard work to crystallize your ideas and be **satisfied** with them. In fact, you will almost rather pick up the telephone and call me.

● Now let me make it easier for you. I am not interested in your handwriting, your English or grammar, spelling, or the way you organize sentences. I am only interested in how you know you are saved. If you put it crudely, that won't matter. I am looking for your heart. Take your time and make yourself the critic—not me.

Don't try to satisfy me with the statement. I don't have to be satisfied, but you do. When you can read what you have written and feel satisfied it tells how you know you are saved, send it to me. I will read it and rejoice. And I will acknowledge it. We will become friends by mail and look forward to meeting in His presence later on. Remember, I am your friend, so don't fuss about the wording or spelling, will you?

59

NOTE: Should this book come into your hands after C. S. Lovett has "graduated," provision will have been made for someone here at Personal Christianity to receive your letter and acknowledge it. And you will receive back something that will help in the witness-life.

REASON

In order to get any idea into words, truths must be organized and processed in one's mind. It is only after it is arranged into words, that it can be transmitted. The hard work of focusing and crystallizing truths pays off. For what was once vague and scattered, now becomes a solid tool. The mental energy that goes into shaping a scattered truth, cements in the understanding. Once a Christian does this with his salvation experience, he can begin the witnessing course with confidence. It is on this healthy foundation that we rest our witnessing ladder.

● SO DO IT. Write to me. Don't call me Dr. Lovett or Rev. Lovett. Call me "C.S." I am your friend now. Once you get that letter on its way, you will have your foot resting on the first rung of the witnessing ladder.

LESSONS: The witnessing ladder has also been prepared as a correspondence course. If you are interested in having me for a personal coach, see details in the back of the book. They show how I teach the course by mail, and let you see the benefit of reporting your action-steps to us here at Personal Christianity.

Ready to go up the ladder? That comes next.

Chapter Six

STARTING UP THE LADDER

There are ten steps (rungs) in our witnessing course. Each offers a bit more ego threat than the preceding one. With people the real threat, we start off with no direct, personal contact. We begin the course with secret actions, gradually moving closer and closer to people in bite-sized experiments that are FUN. That's what makes it easy—increasing the stress in small doses. As soon as a person absorbs all the threat at one level and feels comfortable doing the action, he is ready to advance to the next higher level.

> **NOTE: There is no time limit for this course. Stay on any rung of the ladder as long as necessary. No two people are alike. An action which might be easy and natural for one person, could be a nightmare for another. One witness might have to remain on a step for as long as six months, whereas another could be ready to move on in three weeks. By staying on a particular rung of the ladder until the witnessing is comfortable, you avoid the distressing feeling of being pushed into something beyond you. However, if you are taking this course in a class, follow the teacher's schedule, but plan on spending more time on your own later on so as to bring yourself to full strength on each rung.**

● At first, you'll be tempted to regard the actions as overly simple. You will be right, the actions are indeed simple. But the lessons extracted from doing them are NOT simple. So don't say to yourself, "That's too easy" or "I've done that before," and start skipping steps. Don't be fooled by the simplicity of the assignments. There are powerful forces at work in every action. It is with **these** that we are concerned. Merely going through the motions means nothing. You will be defrauded of insight and strength if you breeze up the rungs, interested only in the **mechanics** of witnessing. There's a big difference between doing actions and building strengths.

OBSERVE: There are Christians witnessing today who do not enjoy their work. They do it out of a sense of duty. They feel they have to. They suffer because they have not learned how much the Holy Spirit is ready to do. They don't know how to RELAX and let Him do His part. Why? They've skipped the early steps, failing to get acquainted with the Holy Spirit and His part in the actions. They know almost nothing of the COMFORT which attends moving in His power. Therefore, I want you to take your time. Don't rush. Draw all you can from each action. Later on you'll be relaxed even though you are on the highest rungs of the ladder. You'll enjoy yourself as you share Christ with others, having acquired the little refinements and skills necessary for working with the Holy Spirit at close range.

Even the most timid, shy Christian can start this plan. The first actions are so stripped of threat, the oldest lady in your church could do them. There's not a saint anywhere who couldn't climb the first three rungs of the ladder. When he does, he'll be amazed at his progress. The strength which comes through doing these actions is astounding. But who knows that until he tries? In time, the witness can look back down the ladder to see how far he has come. Then it strikes him, if he had to cover that distance in one jump, he never would have made it. That's the advantage of following a plan that breaks up the distance into small doses of ego threat.

● Did you write out your salvation experience? It wasn't as easy as it sounded, was it? Even if you can't pinpoint the moment you received Christ, you must be able to say to yourself, "I know I am saved right now, and here's why." His indwelling is a working truth. You must be on intimate terms with Jesus, able to chat with Him about the actions. That is the foundation on which the witnessing-ladder rests. It is the basis of all that is before us as we proceed with the course. From this moment on, I do not want you to think of yourself as witnessing for Christ—but WITH HIM!

LEAVE A TRACT

THE BOTTOM RUNG

Are you ready for spiritual adventure? Good. I am going to describe the first step. You'll smile at the simplicity of the action, but don't let that fool you. It is not as simple as it sounds on the surface. A good beginning is vital to your success as a witness, perhaps even the most critical point. And where will we begin? In the world, of course, for that is where the Great Commission sends us. We will not be doing this action in church. You are going to be leaving a tract—in the world—without letting anyone see you do it.

What's so hard about that, you ask? Nothing. But if you follow my instructions carefully, you'll taste adventure. There's a lot more to witnessing with Jesus in the world than most suspect. There's a whole science of working with the Holy Spirit to be learned. That's what's going to be new. Do not people have glorious experiences with the Spirit in church? Yes, they do. But those experiences have nothing to do with what is before us. Working with the Spirit in the world, to reach the lost, is unlike any experience you might have with the Spirit in church.

So where do we start? We'll begin with what I call the irreducible minimum of obedience to the Great Commission—secretly leaving a tract in a public place. On the surface, what could be easier? But what tract? I want you to select one that you think would be good as a "leaving tract." They are shown in the PC catalog. (If you do not have a catalog, you may send for a free one. See back of book for details.) One tract I like very much is called, "Religion Can Be Dangerous." The title is so provocative. The unsaved bite on it, thinking it supports their disinterest in godly things. Fold

63

a few and place them in your shirt pocket or tract holder. Be sure to have them on your person when you leave the house.

ACTION

1 Stop at a gas station (or restaurant) which has a public restroom offering LOCKED PRIVACY. It must have a door that locks from the **inside**. If it doesn't, you won't have the privacy you need for this exercise. Enter the room. "Click," lock the door behind you. Now you're all alone. No one can get in unless you unlock the door. See how safe you are? There's no way for people to come bursting into the room and discover you in the act of leaving a tract. Theoretically, then, you should be free of all worry. Right?

Now reach to your pocket for a tract. But don't take it out—just yet. Let your hand rest over your heart for a few seconds. Kerplump! Kerplump! Kerplump! Why—your heart is racing! Feel that accelerated beat? How come? You're in the place of fear. You are in the world about to do something **with Jesus.** It doesn't matter that the door is locked. It's still enemy territory. What you are feeling is FEAR. But that's great. If you're going to learn to conquer fear in the power of the Holy Spirit, then you have to be in the **place of fear.**

NOTE: You can see how it would be impossible to do this exercise in church. The church is NOT a place of fear. It's a place of peace and blessing—just the opposite of fear. Therefore, we cannot expect to learn how to overcome fear in a witnessing class in church. Without these feelings, it is impossible to sample the Spirit's might in overcoming them. The world and the church are two different realms. The working of God's Spirit is different in each place. One may indeed thrill to the PRESENCE of God's Spirit in a fellowship of Christians, but it is in the world that His POWER is manifested with the greatest force. We'll see this more clearly as we climb the ladder.

2 Now draw out a tract from your pocket. Hold it out to your side at arm's length. (See photo). It quivers, doesn't it? That quivering is . your fear translated into something you can see. The shaking of your fingers corresponds to the trembling of your heart. The fluttering of that tract is YOUR FEAR out there where you can look at it. The more shy you are the more that tract will shake. The more bold and aggressive you are, the less it will shake. But there will be some feelings for you to deal with.

NOTE: Satan isn't a bit happy to have you serious about serving Christ. He is the author of the fears you feel at this moment. He can intensify dread, so that your heart races when there should be no fear at all. After all, who can get in? The door's locked, and you are secure. A lot of Christians do not believe Satan is real, but their lives are living proof of his power. What you're feeling at this moment is also proof of his presence. Every Christian should equip himself to deal with the devil per the counsel of James 4:7, "Resist the devil and he will flee from you." It is impossible to have dramatic victory in one's life without some skill in putting him to flight. That's why I wrote DEALING WITH THE DEVIL. It provides a 4-step plan for resisting him and ridding yourself of his presence. It can make a mighty difference in one's life, and you could prove the power of such know-how right at this moment, if you had the skill.

3 With your arm **still extended**, bow your head. You are going to speak directly to the Holy Spirit. If you have never done this before, determine to do so now. After all, He is GOD. Ignoring Him is perhaps the greatest sin in the church today, and the real reason behind the decline in the various denominations. So, with your hand still trembling, speak to Him. . .aloud. . .

"God the Holy Spirit, behold my trembling heart, and comfort me now!"

You can say more than that if you like, but the important thing is dealing with Him directly while you are in the place of fear. Don't just mouth those words in a prayer exercise, actually talk TO Him—and make it intimate. What happens next, you see, is up to Him. So move in on Him as prayerfully as you can.

Now look at your hand. It's settling down. Simultaneously you feel a warmth within you. Yes, you sense His protection. He is moving upon your spirit and your awareness of His presence is like armor for your soul. God's own Person settles about you like a shield. At least that's the sensation. Actually it is your AWARENESS of Him that is so comforting. He gives you that. This is why He is called the Comforter.

> **NOTE: This is where the witnessing course really begins— getting acquainted with the Spirit of God in a LIVE situation. This is where He proves Himself to become the fountain of your boldness. Therefore, this is a critical moment. Don't rush it. Extract all the awareness you can from it. If you want to spend a moment or two praising Him for His sweet presence when you need it, do so. But leave your arm out there. I don't want you to bring it back or drop it to your side. You'll see why in the next move.**

Witnessing has to start someplace. A man can't say, "I'm going to be a witness for Christ," and then charge off into the crowds. Only the rarest soul can do that. Ninety-nine out of one hundred Christians have to start at the bottom and work their way up—gradually. Their boldness has to come little by little. Witnessing for Christ is a new way of life for them, and they are not able to begin it with one big blast. That's why we're at the bottom of the ladder, why we're at the minimum action. Since it is a new way of life for the average Christian, we have to start with toddler steps.

It is not an exaggeration to say that today's Christian needs to get acquainted with the Spirit of God—in the world. Few know anything of the way He works through believers to reach the lost around them. What they do know, is theory only. Not one in a thousand has actually sampled the Spirit's might as his own. Christians know about it, but they've never experienced it. Since it is a whole new way of life, the only place to begin is at the beginning. So here you are, experiencing the presence of God's Spirit in a new way as He moves on your soul to strengthen you in a witnessing situation.

> **NOTE: The question could be asked, "Wouldn't the Holy Spirit automatically do this, even if we didn't ask**

Him?" The answer is no. Like anyone else, He hates to be taken for granted. But there's another reason. It was the Lord's intention to win men to Himself by working WITH us. He could do the job by Himself, but for fellowship's sake, He purposed it would be an active partnership. This is the whole point of the Great Commission. If men ignore the Spirit of God or refuse to work closely with Him, they end up working in the flesh. This is why so many are powerless today, why they don't enjoy witnessing to others. It is no FUN for the Lord to be ignored or taken for granted. It would frustrate the entire program if He backed our actions when we pay no attention to Him at all. No, the anointing of the Spirit is NOT automatic. At the very least, we must be watching for it.

● But you have asked. The Comforter has responded. No matter what you thought of the Holy Spirit before, you have now had an EXPERIENCE. You may have even taught the **doctrine** of the Comforter in your church, but now you have **experienced** Him in the world. You have made the important shift from theory to action. See now why I want you to extract all you can from this moment?

NOTE: Most evangelicals own sound doctrine concerning the Holy Spirit, but meeting those doctrines in ACTION can be a surprise. Sadly though, many who are firmly settled in the truth of God's Spirit, are not able to recognize that same truth when it occurs right in front of their eyes. That's why this simple exercise is so necessary. When a Christian suddenly sees his doctrine in action, he enjoys an EXPERIENCE. But until he has that experience, his doctrine remains as theory only. It is one thing, you see, to believe the Holy Spirit is a Comforter, quite another to experience His COMFORT when you need it. So it is with all of the Holy Spirit's ministries.

4 Now swing your arm so that you can place the tract on a towel box or shelf. It really doesn't matter where, so long as it is in plain view of anyone who might enter the room after you. As the tract leaves your fingers, say aloud. . .

"In the name of the Lord Jesus Christ!"

That's for your benefit. I told you this was the beginning point. For some this will be the first time they have ever **declared** Jesus' name in a public place. Here is this private moment you can taste the thrill of it. Be bold as you say it. No one can get in. Try and sense the delight that goes with having that precious name on your lips. You're sure to like it. It will prepare you to utter His name a bit more publicly later on.

> NOTE: Again don't be in a hurry. Even though this beginning exercise is done in secret, there is an anointing that goes with it. I want you to discover it. No one is watching. Though you make your motions deliberately, I want you to focus on the Spirit rather than your action. Be conscious of Him even as your hand deposits the tract and your lips speak that Holy name. You can do that here. If you were trying this in a more public situation, you'd be so worried about someone seeing you, the Holy Spirit's working would be overshadowed. You wouldn't detect it. You see, His voice and His moves are so unfamiliar to you at first, you really have to be looking for them. Once you

catch on to what you're looking for, it is easier and His voice gets louder. But right now, you must take your time and extract all you can from this private moment. It is more vital than I can say.

5 Unlock the door. Leave the room. Run, if you feel like it. As you go your way, check your heart once more. Is it fearful now? Indeed not. The fear has been replaced with JOY. You feel it. In fact you are a little flush. It's no small thing to meet the Holy Spirit like that and find Him ready to bless even the tiniest thing you do in Jesus' name. Your heart pounds a little wildly as you realize this prepares you for the next thing you're going to do in His name.

NOTE: Why is your heart so joyful? Is it due merely to sampling the supernatural? Indeed not. While that is no slight matter, you have just learned another lesson— OBEDIENCE BRINGS BLESSING. What you are feeling is the joy of the Lord. That's God's own pleasure echoing in your soul. He gets thrills too. You just handed Him one.

He's overjoyed to see you in action, serious about investing your life in obedience to His command. Though you have merely put your foot on the first rung of the ladder, it offers as much promise to Him as it does to you. He can look forward to having lots of good times with you. The pleasure of God is not just a doctrine. You can experience it, too. That's His "well done" you're feeling in your heart right now.

BUT IT'S SO SIMPLE. . .!

Is that notion still buzzing in your mind? Granted, the exercise is simple, but it is too vital to skip. I guarantee your witnessing will never be what it should, if you bypass this action. There are too many urgent lessons to be extracted from it. Others who have skipped this assignment are not the faithful and joyous witnesses they should be. For those who mean business for Christ, this is the first major step into the witness life.

To be a relaxed, powerful witness for Jesus, **and love every minute of it,** demands this intimate acquaintance with the Holy Spirit. Taste it once, and you'll want more. To satisfy yourself, let's go back and see again the rich things which happen when you complete this assignment:

a. You become acquainted with God's Spirit IN THE WORLD. That's the very place the Great Commission sends us. Witnessing to others isn't nearly so frightening when we learn BY EXPERIENCE that the Holy Spirit is ready to back all we do and say in Jesus' name. To find Him ALIVE and eager to be your strength gives you your first boost in boldness.

b. By experience you learn that FEAR can be overcome in the POWER of the Holy Spirit. You may have heard that before, but until now it was in your mind as **theory** only. Now the event has happened. You have met the exciting difference between theory and action. It could only happen here. Therefore, the overcoming of fear in God's power is not something which can be acquired at church or in a witnessing class. The proper laboratory for witnessing to the lost is in the world itself.

c. You enjoy locked privacy. Unless you are totally secure in this action, your mind will be occupied with the threat of discovery. The threat of someone coming in and discovering you doing this exercise could desensitize your mind to the Spirit's working. He would still do His part, but you wouldn't be aware of it. The threat is so overpowering, it sweeps your mind clear of everything else. There is no way to sample those first feelings of God's presence in a witnessing situation without secure privacy in a public place. Only by doing as I have outlined, will you be able to relax and concentrate on the Spirit.

d. There are glorious feelings that go with declaring Jesus' name in a public place. But where does one start getting such experience? Where better than here in this secure restroom? Those precious feelings would be wiped out by threat were you in a place where someone might walk in on you. No, locked privacy is absolutely essential. Everybody who fearlessly speaks out for Jesus has to begin somewhere. The easier we can make that beginning, the more people we can activate for Christ.

e. Then there is the JOY that obedience brings. This tiny exercise brings God's "well done" to your soul. There's a delightful intoxication that goes with it, and you're sure to want more. This one sample is enough to convince any Christian that he should devote himself to obeying the Lord. The Spirit-filled man is one who is high on the Holy Spirit. The secret of being Spirit-filled is getting hooked on the blessing that obedience brings. You get your first taste with this exercise.

f. You have done an action WITH the Lord in the world. That's what the Great Commission is all about. Jesus said

72

"Go. . .and lo I am with you always. . ." (Matt. 28:19,20). That word "WITH" is so vital. The difference between witnessing FOR the Lord and WITH Him is like night and day. The action you have just completed was calculated to make you aware of His presence as you performed the step. It must be like that with every action in the future. The Lord does not want to be left out of the witnessing program. He never intended for us to do ONE THING without Him (John 15:5). However, the business of witnessing **with** Christ is a new ball game for the average Christian. Many who are witnessing FOR Jesus today, have yet to discover the joy of doing it WITH Him.

• That should erase any thought that this action is not worth doing because it appears so simple. Are you aware that most of the Christians you know have not done this much for Christ, outside the church? It's true. A good many who are churchy, have not stirred themselves to obey the Lord's command. The Great Commission sends no one to church. It orders all of us into the world. Yet, the average Christian is at a loss to know what to do for Christ once he passes out the front door of his church into the world. Here before us is the one action that could activate a host of God's people. It is simple enough for the feeblest, yet effective enough that men like Billy Graham should do it.

LET'S TALK ABOUT YOUR TRACT

You left that slip of paper with its Christian invitation in the restroom. You have no idea what will become of it. Does it seem strange committing such an insignificant thing to the Spirit for Him to use? Let's talk about that before I give you more actions on the first rung of the ladder.

We live in a day when the gospel can be compressed into a few hundred words on a piece of paper. That's a real advantage in this "hit and run" age. People don't have time for sermons any more. They're too busy with other things. This fact has

73

brought the tract into its own, making it a superb weapon of the Holy Spirit for reaching the masses who mill about without Christ. If you have tended to discount the tract ministry, thinking it was "baby-stuff," there are a couple of things you should know.

1. Tracts are like bullets.

They strike their target with terrific impact. The better ones have but a single idea. That's what makes them so perfect for today. When a reader meets that truth, it slams into his spirit with stabbing force. It's not easy to escape a truth once it has been lodged in your understanding. The more simply that truth is presented, the better.

Consider the prospect who sits down in an air terminal. Or perhaps he is on a bus or in a hotel lobby. He notices a slip of paper in the next seat. Maybe it fell out of the magazine he picked up. His eyes spot the engaging cover. He reaches for it. The title is provocative too. Nothing about it betrays its spiritual content. He is intrigued. He begins to read. In seconds his heart is pierced with the truth of Christ. Once he has read God's invitation, his soul is infected with his need for salvation. He will never be able to get away from the truth once it starts working in his mind.

All that is necessary is getting the unsaved man to read one good tract that tells him HOW to be saved. That gives the Holy Spirit a foothold on his soul. The "Hound of Heaven" will take over and track that man using that one truth to dog his steps. There is no way to flee from God's Spirit. It is meeting the truth of Christ in an unusual place that gives the Spirit a big edge. The prospect begins to wonder, "Is God trying to tell me something?" That feature cannot be duplicated in any type of ministry.

2. Tracts can reach masses of unchurched people.

Some years ago there was an aspirin commercial on TV that went like this. "Please mother, I'd rather do it myself!" Commedians picked up the phrase, and people all over began saying, "I'd rather do it myself." Now that line isn't particularly funny. But it is true to human nature. When it comes to salvation, a multitude of people is just like that.

There are those who won't let anyone lead them to Christ. They refuse to come to the Lord, unless it is their own idea. They will not listen to a Christian broadcast, enter a church, or discuss spiritual matters with an evangelical Christian. Their common defense is, **"I don't believe in discussing religion or politics."** How many are like that? Millions. With their minds closed to all PUBLIC means for declaring the gospel, all that is left is the private door. That private door is opened when an unsaved man picks up your unsuspicious tract in an out of the way place.

Now don't be shocked when I tell you that MOST of the people you see daily are like that. This means they are NOT going to be reached any other way. Look around you the next time you are on the job or in some public place. Do you see concern for Christ anywhere? Are there excited groups here and there speaking of the Lord? Indeed not. Mention of the Lord brings scornful glances. He is all but excluded from this world. Even church attendance is reaching an all time low. The great apostasy prophesied by the apostle Paul is at hand. The tract ministry is now the ideal way for gleaning those who will come to Jesus, if they can find Him for themselves. Tracts alone provide the private door to salvation.

A man sits alone in a restaurant booth. He reaches for a packet of sugar for his coffee. But some faithful Christian has carefully concealed a folded tract between the sugar packets. It falls out on the table before the prospect. He sees the provocative title. What else will he do but read it? There, in that private moment, he "discovers" the truth of Christ for Himself. For a few vital seconds the Holy Spirit holds that man's heart in His hands.

It is very possible the Lord had such a scene in mind when He gave His disciples the parable of the hidden-treasure:

> **"Now the kingdom of heaven is like a treasure hid in a field; the which when a man has found it, and for the joy thereof goes and sells all he has and buys that field"** (Matt. 13:44).

Have you ever thought of the "discovered" tract as part of God's "hidden-treasure" program? He uses the "hiding-finding" principle continually. Indeed the best things of life are **always concealed** that life may be a perpetual inquest. God HIDES things that men may have the **joy of finding** them. The "hidden treasure" principle elevates the tract ministry to its proper place. The moment we secretly deposit the printed invitation to Christ, we are employing one of God's FAVORITE methods for reaching men. The more so when you consider some cannot be reached any other way.

3. Tracts never die.

A young marine was about to embark from the United States. His girl friend, concerned for his soul, slipped a tract into his foot locker. It stayed there unnoticed during months of travels about the world. It was still there when he returned to the states a year and a half later. One day, while rumaging through the trunk, he came across the tract. He paused to read it. It touched his conscience to the place where he accepted Christ as his Savior.

Unlike a sermon which vanishes into the air once the words are spoken, a tract can accompany a soul to the far corners of the earth to await the right moment for speaking to his heart. It doesn't care where it rests or might have to hide while awaiting the opportunity. Men have picked up wet and scarred tracts off the streets and have been saved. Janitors have found them in wastebaskets and have been saved. Hudson Taylor, the great missionary, was brought to Christ through finding a tract hidden in one of his father's books.

I read of a diver who was saved at the bottom of the sea. He saw a piece of paper waving in the currents. A closer look revealed it was clutched in the mouth of an oyster fixed on a rock. Curious, he detached it and began to read the message through his face piece. It was a gospel tract. The circumstances were so unusual he sensed God was dealing with him. Later he testified:

"I couldn't hold out against God any longer. His mercy was so great, He caused His Word to follow me to the bottom of the ocean. I was so struck by this I opened my heart to Jesus right then and there."

● Having just said how effectively the Spirit uses tracts today, let me now shock you—**we don't care about the results.** Does that startle you? Good. I said it that way purposely. Of course we care about souls, that's the point of the Commission. But for the purpose of this course, we are interested in YOU and the development of your strengths. You see, God is the real soul-winner anyway, but He needs people. Today very few serve Him with any strength at all.

Therefore, we are concentrating on you and the development of your strengths. If we can make you strong in spirit, plenty of people will be reached for Christ. Consequently, we are not so concerned with what happens to the tract after you leave the restroom. Your part was seeing that it was left in a choice place for the Holy Spirit to use. That's where your responsibility ends.

Are you familiar with the verse:

"Moreover it is required in stewards that a man be found faithful?" (1 Cor. 4:2).

In the course we will be more concerned with your faithfulness as a witness than with the results. Your part is to BE the witness, God's part is to USE it. If you are faithful as a witness, that's all that matters. It's true, of course, that part of that faithfulness is making sure the Holy Spirit has your best for His use. You have just done that with your first action.

1. You selected what you thought was the best tract for the situation.

2. You placed it in a perfect spot for reaching a prospect.

3. You committed the tract and your action to the Lord for His use.

What happens next is up to God's spirit. Your part is done. You have been faithful to do the action, and God is pleased. He will bless it, you can be sure of that.

● The dedicated witness never leaves his house without a number of tracts on his person. Such a thing is unthinkable today when tracts do such a fabulous job. But again, it is what happens to you as a faithful Christian that concerns us. You'll be amazed at the way consistent witnessing keeps your mind on the Lord. Therefore, the more **faithfully** you witness, the closer you find yourself drawn to Him.

Now that you have broken the ice with the "shake test," plan on visiting the restroom each time you go to a restaurant or wheel into a gas station. It takes but a few moments to do this, and they are such important crossroads in your private world. There is a segment of humanity you reach this way, which cannot be reached by any other means. Most restrooms offer locked privacy, but that won't matter much after you have done this a few times. About your fourth or fifth time out, you'll begin to feel like a professional. As you find yourself headed toward the restroom, chat with the Holy Spirit. When it comes time to deposit that tract, you'll have all the boldness you need.

Let's move to another "Leave a Tract" action that can increase your strength a bit more. Naturally it will have a little more threat. Instead of a restroom, this next time we go to a. . .

PHONE BOOTH

You can hardly go anyplace today without seeing a phone booth nearby. Is one convenient to your job or where you shop? Once you discover what wonderful outposts they are for the gospel, you might choose such a booth for a personal mission station. If you pass it often, you could make sure a tract is placed every time you go by. Now for your first action in a phone booth.

ACTION

This time I suggest you leave the tract, "A Penny For Your Thoughts." You'll see why in a moment. Enter the booth. First take out your tract and place it on the coin shelf just below the phone. Then reach into your pocket for a shiny penny. Put the penny on the coin photo on the cover. Then take down the receiver and put it to your ear. Dial the letters J-E-S-U-S. That keeps you from forgetting the most important part—chatting with the Lord. Close your eyes and pray directly into the mouth piece. You can do this aloud if you like. Thank the Lord for His comforting presence. Ask Him to use the tract for His glory. Then hang up and leave the booth.

See how normal that is? Anyone watching you would not suspect your action at all. You took a slip of paper from your pocket. To someone else it merely contained the number you wanted to dial. Then you laid down a coin. People often have to arrange their change in a phone booth. Then you dialed and talked to someone at the other end, or so it seemed. After that you replaced the receiver and left the booth.

There is nothing suspicious about that. Yet you have left a most provocative witness for Christ behind you. Read the tract sample in your catalog. It's a good one. Consider the penny placed on top of it. That increases the provocation 100 times. Sure it's an insignificant amount, but it represents money. And money attracts attention—even a penny.

I recall a time when I lingered to watch the result of leaving this in a booth. A lady walked in, deposited her dime and began to dial. Then she spied the tract with the penny. She instantly halted her dialing, replaced the receiver, and picked up the coin and the tract. First, she looked at the penny, then the tract. She put down the penny and began to read. I began to pray. Now for the punch line. She never made her call, but put the tract in her purse and left the booth. We don't know what action God interrupted there, but He used that penny and tract combination to change the woman's mind about her call. I was aware of seeing the power of God before my eyes.

NOTE: When you are beginning the witness-life, the tendency is to project your feelings onto a possible observer. By that I mean, you believe anyone who happens to see you is thinking to himself, "There's another of those religious nuts." But that is ALMOST NEVER the case. The last thing any spectator wants to do is connect your action with God. Why? It is too painful for a sinner to think of God in any way or of you as His representative. Most always, anyone who views your action will give it other than a spiritual interpretation. If you boldly opened the directory in plain sight of everyone, inserted your tract and then closed the book, do you know what people would think? They'd be certain you had placed your business card in there or some other form of personal advertising. Most of the fears of the witnessing Christian are absolutely groundless.

• Should you go through the dialing scene each time you want to leave a tract in a phone booth? Of course not. It is merely a technique, a crutch for getting you started. It is designed to help you over those first time fears. Yes, you will use it a few times, but it won't be long before you realize others are paying no attention to what you are doing. Chances are, if someone were staring right at you, they wouldn't notice your action. That's how pre-occupied people are with themselves these days.

In time you will be able to go down a whole row of phone booths, say in a drug store or air terminal, with the confidence of a telephone official. You won't even bother to see if anyone is watching, for you know your actions will hardly be interpreted as a spiritual act. The very worst anyone might suspect is that you were passing out political propaganda. Certainly no one cares enough these days to ask you what you're doing. Once you become aware of this **by experience,** it will be hard for you to pass up a phone booth anyplace.

CAUTION: Though we are systematically increasing your boldness and strength, it is vital that you learn to leave tracts in non-suspicious moves. I'm serious about this. We are enemy agents as far as this world is concerned, secret agents for Christ. We need to operate with the skill of commandos as we move about in our private world for Christ. Therefore, you must not let your increased skill and confidence cause you to be careless or cocky. It is urgent that you learn to make obvious moves, yet keep them entirely free of suspicion. That takes practice. It will come only after lots of time in the field. I, myself, can deposit tracts all over a store, clearly in the sight of everyone, and no one thinks anything of it because I have learned to do so without making suspicious moves. You'll have that skill too, before we're through.

After you have done the phone booth exercise a dozen times, you will have absorbed much of the threat which accompanys the action. Then you'll be ready for something more daring—something like leaving a tract on the table or counter when you leave a restaurant.

TIPPING WITH TRACTS

This time I am going to ask you to leave a tract with your tip the next time you dine out. Right off you can see the increase in threat. The waitress who finds the tract knows YOU left it. You may think to yourself, "Oh, I could never do that." But you'll change your mind when you see the special tracts designed to help you. We have two that are excellent for this purpose, "Thank You" and "Here's a Tip."

The "Thank You" tract strips away most of the threat because it is a courtesy before it is a witness. People appreciate being thanked. And certainly no one objects to having it in writing. Having a functional tract like this makes the action less threatening than it might be otherwise. Still, you will be doing a witnessing action in public. Even though no one is to see you do it, it still remains a public witness. Saying thank you with a tract is itself a novelty. If your tip should come to a dollar, and you place it inside the tract (letting the ends of the bill show), it is even more welcome.

If your tip calls for coins, then use the "Tip" tract. Place your coins on the cover, and it will add to the novelty. Again we harness the principle of provocation as we did with the "Penny" tract in the phone booth. Waiters are very interested in their tips, and that fascination is unconsciously transferred to your

82

printed message. I assure you there is not a single unpleasant reaction generated by leaving a tract in this manner. To the contrary, those who serve tables like the novelty of it. It breaks up the monotony for one thing.

ACTION

I understand you will have fears when you try this for the first time. But that's good. The threat is one you can handle. You're ready for it now. Strength comes as we try the next harder action. So now you have finished your meal. It's time to leave. This is the moment to speak to the Holy Spirit. "Lord, strengthen me with Your presence right now, even as You have before." Then carefully slip your tract holder (if you're using one by now) from your purse or pocket and drop it into your lap. **Remember: no one is to see you do this.**

Just before you rise from the table, ease the tract up from your lap under the rim of your plate. Then go and pay your check, or leave the restaurant if the bill has already been taken care of, whichever the case may be.

There now, that wasn't so bad, was it? Take my word for it. Your waitress will not be offended when she finds your tract with the tip. You'll be asking yourself, "What's so hard about that?" And then, before long, it will be a habit to leave a tract behind every time you eat out.

On numerous occasions I have purposely stationed myself outside a restaurant where I could watch the person who picked up the tip and the tract. More than once I have seen a waitress pick up the money and put it in her pocket. Then, as she wiped off the table with one hand, she read the tract with the other. That's one reason why we print them with so little copy. Your waitress can read the entire message before she leaves your table. That's an advantage in this jet age.

• After this action you will find your strength has moved up quite a bit. After you have used the "Tip" or "Thank You" tracts half-a-dozen times, you'll be delighted with the advance in your public strength. You're a little bolder now than you were a couple of weeks ago. It's not a giant advance, but it's an important one. Remember, we're going from strength to strength, so each advance becomes the platform for the next one. When you have done this ten times, most of the threat will have been absorbed.

COMBINED ACTION

As the practice of leaving tip tracts becomes some-what routine, you will find yourself adding to the witness. While waiting to be served, a trip to the rest-room is in order. Ask the Lord to bless the tract you're going to leave there. Then deposit it atop the towel dispenser where the Holy Spirit can direct His prospect to it. When you return to the table, see if there is a napkin dispenser. Conceal a tract in it about 3 or 4 napkins back. Are there sugar packets in a bowl? Good. A folded "Curious" tract fits perfectly among them and looks almost like a packet itself. Then as you leave let your hand flop a tract on top of the self-service newspaper bin, if there is one in front of the restaurant. You'll find you can do this in a single, casual motion which is fully free of all suspicion.

NOTE: Witnessing muscle does not come much faster than body muscle. Both require faithful exercise if there is to be dramatic improvement. Progress is slow. If you've ever worked with weights, you know it takes time to harden muscle. Witnessing muscle, you see, is not a matter of acquiring techniques. It has to do with a CHANGE in your strength. True, you are acquiring know-how and skills, but they are useless by themselves. It is only as your personality strengths increase that you become effective for Christ. A witness is a CHANGED man, not one who has merely learned some moves. Please see that. That's why I don't want you to rush through the course. Give yourself time to change. Watch for advances in boldness as your personality gets stronger. Enjoy it. It is fascinating to see YOURSELF move more gracefully toward people. Stay with it. In time you won't recognize your old self. You will become a more outgoing person. Why? Constant action toward others makes us that way.

● We've spent a lot of time on the first rung of the ladder. But it is important to get off to a good start. It can make a lot of difference in the steps ahead. As soon as you have completed the three different actions: (1) shake test, (2) phone booth, (3) leaving "Tip" tracts, you will have met the requirements for STEP ONE of the witnessing ladder. You can move on to Rung No. 2 if you like.

OTHER PLACES FOR TRACTS

Leaving tracts is such a fertile way of reaching souls, I must list other places in your private world. You don't have to try them now, if you don't want to. You can wait until you feel stronger. But please consider them.

1. Parking lots

People don't even walk to the corner any more. America moves on wheels. Department stores and shopping centers are not allowed to build unless they provide huge parking areas. The empty, parked cars of shoppers provide ideal places for tracts, in warm weather especially. As an easy beginning, start disciplining yourself NOT to park close to the entrance of the market or store. The walk will be good for you, besides, there will be lots of cars between you and the store in which you wish to shop. I know that means breaking an old habit, for it is most natural to park as close to the store as you can.

Park your car. Is there a car next to you? Is the window open? Toss a tract inside on the seat. There, isn't that easy? Maybe there will be several with open windows between you and the store entrance. Try getting tracts in one or two.

Then after you have done this a few times, it would be an increase in boldness to place one under the windshield wiper of the car next to you. If you have come there in the evening, then let the darkness cover your action. Try reaching a few more cars. On a warm summer evening, you will find you can deposit as many as 30 to 50 tracts in this fashion in a single parking lot. In time, you will become resourceful, developing ingenious ways for fitting tracts in door cracks and windows.

> HINT: As your skill mounts and your strength also rises, you will find yourself reaching possibly 100 cars in a single outing like this. But again, be cautious. Without looking around, know where the pedestrians or security guards (if any) are. Don't let yourself be spotted. That's part of the technique. If a store manager or policeman asks you what you are doing, be ready with your answer. "I have a message for these people that I think is so important to them, that I have taken the trouble to see that they get it at my own expense." You'll get a polite "Oh," followed by a request that you not do it any more. Agree quickly. Make no defense whatsoever. Then comply. You'll have to figure it was your own fault you got caught. The penalty is the forfeiture of a nice mission station. Fortunately, there are others.

2. Libraries

In the 200 section of the public library are books on religion and philosophy. The first time out you might feel a bit timid. If so, select a book and take it to a reading table. Notice where the book falls open. That's the place to conceal "Religion Can Be Dangerous," "You Ought to Reject Christ," or "How to get Rid of Religious Fanatics." If you find a book on evolution, then use the tract, "Monkey Business." Anyone seeing this action would assume you were inserting a bookmark. As you replace the book, chat with the Holy Spirit. He has a sense of humor, you know. He is going to have some FUN with the prospect who finds that tract. If you experience a deep chuckle inside you, that will be the Holy Spirit laughing.

After you have done this a few times, you may wish to move among the stacks salting one book after another. Be sure to commit each to the Spirit of God. He wants to be in on every action. If the librarian should catch you, don't try to lie your way out. It will damage your spirit to use the lie as a defensive maneuver. Simply say, "I felt this item would be of such interest to the next person reading this book, I was willing to include it at my own expense." Work on your skill so that you will not be caught. The library is a well-traveled cross road in your private world. Those who use it are usually thinkers.

3. Doctor's offices.

In most waiting rooms there are tables with reading materials. You can easily pick up a magazine and while scanning through it, drop a tract into the fold and then return it to the table and select another. As in the library anyone seeing your action would think you had inserted a bookmark. There isn't a lot of threat in this action. Practice it at home a couple of times before you go to the doctor. There you can perfect the easiest way to bring out your tract and get it into the magazine. See, there is more to leaving tracts than appears on the surface.

4. Stores.

We could spend a long time on this one. For those who develop the skill of leaving tracts in public crossroads, stores provide a multitude of wonderful places for concealing tracts. But you must not get caught. Determine to become a top agent for Christ. For this action we use a tract that folds down to a small size permitting a number of them to be carried unnoticed in the palm of the hand.

The tract I suggest is the one called "Curious." You can read the sample in the catalog to see that it speaks of recovering a huge inheritance because of discovering a folded piece of paper. There's intrigue in the tract itself. Before you set out for your trip to the store, be sure you have a supply of these on your person.

HINT: Do you watch TV? Make that time count for Christ by folding your tracts as you sit in front of the set. In fact, that's one way to justify some of the time normally lost through watching television. The "Curious" tract has three folds at least. Some witnesses prefer a four-fold method. If you fold about 50 of them in one evening that should last you for several outings to a large discount house or department store.

Here are some of the places within a department store where you could use this tract:

a. When trying on a jacket or coat, shove your hand into the pocket and leave the tract when you withdraw your hand.

b. If you are a lady, it is a simple matter to examine purses and, as ladies will do, run your hand inside the purse. Again, leave the tract.

c. If you try on clothes in a dressing room, it is simple to leave a tract behind. You have the place to yourself. The next person will find it if it jauntily beckons him to the accessory shelf.

d. When trying on slippers or shoes in a self-service department, run your hand inside the shoe and leave the tract. No one can see this action at all.

e. Go to the small appliance section. See the waffle irons, coffee makers, etc., all with their instructions? Place your tract with the instructions. You can do the same when it comes to vacuum cleaners or sewing machines, etc.

f. If you visit the furniture department, a tract could be left under the cushion, where you slide your hand to get the feel of the material. You can innocently run your hand inside a desk or dresser drawer, leaving a tract behind.

g. If you browse the book section or check the albums in the music department, you will find all kinds of places for concealing tracts.

h. In most household sections there are packages that customers frequently pick up and examine before buying. Consider a package of light bulbs, for example. You could examine a pack, insert the tract, and return it to the shelf without making one suspicious move—provided the tract is already in the palm of your hand.

i. Stop at the magazine section. If others are around, so much the better. There's less chance anyone will pay attention to you. Develop the skill of picking up a magazine, letting your tract fall into the fold and then returning it. With a little practice, you can do this so smoothly, your action is practically undetectable. Try it at home first.

. . .and so on.

With a little thought, you can turn up all sorts of places that are ideal for concealing tracts.

CONCEAL: That is the key word. Do not scatter tracts throughout a store. That is, do not leave them on top of shelves or lying exposed on goods. Store personnel will merely scoop them up. If you do much of it they will start watching for you. Besides most managers resent it. If

this is a shop or center that you visit regularly, then it is even more important that you conceal your tract, so as to protect your mission station. But that's not the only reason for concealing your tract. When a tract is discovered later by a purchaser, he is struck by the unusual way God has reached him. Not only does the tract get a better reading, the element of "discovery" adds a useful emotion.

• I'm serious about wanting you to become a top agent for Christ. There's nothing make-believe about it. It's serious business for those who take Jesus' Word seriously. The rewards are high for those who mean business about the Great Commission. Not all of us can enter the ministry as a profession, but we can all become professional about reaching our private world for Christ. I want you to be professional. That's why I've written this book. Wouldn't you like to be able to say to yourself, "My profession is witnessing for Christ!"

Let me tell you about a professional Christian. His name is Jack. He is one of the directors of Personal Christianity. He works in a multi-story office building in Beverly Hills. It is owned by his company, a 2.7 billion dollar concern, and he is a vice-president. So you know he is a professional as far as the world is concerned.

We're going to follow Jack as he goes to lunch on a typical day. I won't mention his person to person contacts. At this point we're concerned only with the way he reaches his private world with tracts. Before he leaves the office, he invites the Lord Jesus to go to lunch with him and give him boldness for his witnessing ministry.

As he steps into the elevator, his hand is already reaching for an "Elevator" tract (See tract no. 421 in the catalog.) No one sees his action. His arm drops to his side. He hangs the tract over the hand rail. When he walks from the elevator, there it is, waiting for a prospect to see it and be attracted.

In the lobby he pauses at the cigarette machines. Not to buy anything, of course, but to leave a tract in the discharge chute. His action is totally non-suspicious. Then he checks the phone booths, placing a tract in each before walking out of the building. He doesn't drive to lunch. He walks that he might place tracts on cars along the sidewalk. At the restaurant he checks the newspaper racks outside. If he has to wait in the foyer for the hostess to seat him, he busys himself concealing tracts in the diner's club applications and folders that are often displayed in restaurants. After securing his table, he visits the restroom and phone booths. While waiting to be served he salts the sugar and napkin dispensers.

When the menu has a string down the center, he places a tract in the fold so that the string holds it in place. Naturally he leaves a tract with his tip, and sometimes there's an opportunity to conceal one in the items about the cashier's stand. Then he heads back to the office, catching any cars missed before. Before taking the elevator, he checks the phone booths and cigarette machines. If his tracts are gone, he replaces them. At night, he manages to place tracts on some of the cars in the company garage. Jack tells me it is a rare day when he places fewer than 50 tracts.

Now why do I tell this story? Jack is a professional Christian. He is business-like in his service for Christ. Yet, all of his action is done within the course of his normal routine. Don't miss that. That's what builds the witnessing habit. It is this day in and day out faithfulness within our daily cycle that makes us effective for Christ and draws us closer to Him. It is being business-like about witnessing that finally changes us.

CAUTION: Get rid of any notion that leaving tracts is "baby-stuff" and should be reserved for the beginning Christian. The opposite is true. The further one progresses with Christ, the more he should appreciate the need for reaching the "unreachables" of his private world. Even Billy Graham should leave tracts as part of his daily routine.

True, he ministers to millions publically, but there are many in his private world who cannot be reached any other way. So don't think to yourself, "There now, I've done Step One. I'll now leave that action and go to the next rung." No matter how far up the witnessing ladder you climb, you must always leave tracts. There is no substitute for this action.

We have stayed on this rung a long time. Why? For the average Christian, whose spiritual service is limited to church-going or some job in a church, the actions I have described here in step one sound like a whole new world. It is a new world, particularly for the person who thought living a "good life" was the way to witness for Christ. For such a Christian to discover that he hasn't even started to obey the Lord can be a shock. Getting started, can be an even bigger shock. Therefore, I felt it was important to take this much time to open the door of the new world of the Great Commission.

Also, I know from experience, that a host of readers will go no farther up the ladder. They will learn the skill of leaving tracts and there it stops. That means their outreach for Christ will be limited to this first rung. For them it is still a 100% improvement. They will have gone from dis-obedience to a wonderful method of reaching those about them. Since that is going to be the limit of their involvement with the Great Commission, I want them to be as professional as they can. If they will set themselves to become TOP agents on the first rung, they can enjoy a fabulous ministry to their own private world.

Anyone who begins reaching his private world like this is already a 100% success in God's eyes. But begin is the right word. We have just begun. Of course, I won't be spending anywhere near this amount of time on RUNG No. 2. We come to that, next.

Chapter Seven

TRACTS IN LETTERS

Wasn't I correct? Obedience does bring blessing, doesn't it? You are in action, sampling the first delights that come from obeying the Great Commission. Yes, your moves are secretive. But that's what makes it easy to get started with the witness-life. And now you and the Holy Spirit are becoming more intimate as the two of you leave tracts here and there in Jesus' name.

You must continue to leave tracts even though you are ready for the next step up the witnessing ladder. It is so effective for reaching your private world, you must not stop. Plan to do it in addition to what you will learn in this second lesson. In fact, everything you learn in this book should be carried on continuously by the dedicated Christian.

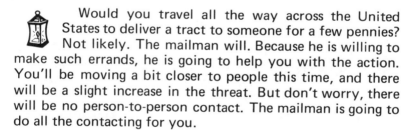

Would you travel all the way across the United States to deliver a tract to someone for a few pennies? Not likely. The mailman will. Because he is willing to make such errands, he is going to help you with the action. You'll be moving a bit closer to people this time, and there will be a slight increase in the threat. But don't worry, there will be no person-to-person contact. The mailman is going to do all the contacting for you.

NOTE: How grateful we should be to Johann Gutenberg. Until the advent of the printing press with moveable type, there was no way to reduce the gospel to leaflets as we have them today. Now we can compress Jesus' invitation into an exciting tract. We can choose every word carefully, making sure it is just right for the unsaved reader. What a privilege to have such a tool to use for the Lord. Tracts are simply great. They say only what they are supposed to say, and no one can argue with them. With each passing day, they become more effective for gleaning souls as we move into the end time.

THREAT AND DISTANCE

On this rung of the ladder, you will begin reaching souls in your private world in a more personal way. Still there is no face-to-face threat, for you enjoy the safety of distance. Doesn't that sound nice? On the first rung, you left tracts for people to find. This time you will mail them to people of **your choice**. That makes it a genuine advance over the first rung. And since the people know the tract has come from you, there is also an increase in threat. You are going to be identified with the tract. If a receiver wanted to, he could even ask you about it. That's what makes this action more threatening.

We are going to break up that threat into two separate doses. Your first tracts will not go to people you know. Therefore, there will be two different types of mailings on this rung of the ladder. Consistent with our plan for easing closer and closer to people, your first assignment will be to mail tracts to INSTITUTIONS. Institutions, while they employ people, are far more impersonal. It is less threatening to send a letter with a tract to a public utility, for example, than to some individual you know.

FIRST ASSIGNMENT

See tract number 403 in the catalog. It is called "Bills, Bills, Bills." Everyone has those. Read it. See how it starts off? "I like paying bills." Suppose you were a cashier or receiving clerk in a public utility, and this tract fell out of a payment envelope. You'd see that title, "Bills, Bills, Bills." Wouldn't you be curious? You bet. You couldn't help but pick it up and begin to read. And imagine your feelings when you came to those words, "I like paying bills!" That would be a shocker. The idea is so unusual, it would thrust itself into your thought process. Before long the truth of Christ paying that big bill would be firmly lodged in your mind.

Bill paying is part of your routine, right? We all pay bills. If we can harness the ritual of bill-paying to a gospel tract, we tap another segment of our private world for Christ. Surely the Great Commission extends to that tiny corner of our private world as it does to any other. Let's face it, there is no area in our lives that is exempt from the Lord's ownership. The very fact that we are His servants makes it plain that His Lordship reaches right down into a matter as tiny as paying our bills.

● Go to your desk or wherever you keep your unpaid bills. If it is a desk, think of it as a sort of pulpit. From this little outpost you can reach lots of people. And it is so convenient to keep tracts at hand in a drawer. As you look about, is there a bill due? Can you afford to pay it? If so, address an envelope right now. Put a "Bills" tract inside. That will get you into action.

Now make out your check. As you are about to seal the envelope, lift your heart to the Holy Spirit. Say to Him something like this:

A MISSILE SET FOR THE TARGET!

95

"Lord may it please you to have someone picked out to receive this tract. Bless it to his heart as he reads."

Then go to the mailbox. As you stand there about to let the envelope drop from your fingers, pause. Don't let go of it just yet. What are your feelings now when you realize the person at the other end is going to know YOU are the one who sent the tract? The moment that thought comes to mind, you will feel the threat that comes with this exercise. It's real.

NOTE: Just before that envelope slips from your fingers, one of two thoughts will come to mind: "What will they think of me? Probably that I'm some sort of a fanatic" or "Lord, I'm excited about what you might do with this. I sure hope you can get it to the right person." One of those thoughts will be inspired by the Holy Spirit, the other by the unholy spirit, Satan. You have moved and so has the devil. It is by the power of such suggestions that Satan can idle the host of God's people. When you come right down to it, what does it matter what the receiver thinks? Your strength as a witness rises as you begin to care more about what Jesus thinks, than what others think.

Do you see why I would have you pause before dropping that letter? Two things will surface in your mind if you do this in slow motion: (1) the threatening idea of what the person receiving the tract will think of you, (2) the desire to do God's will as you set yourself to obey the Great Commission. One of those ideas will be more powerful than the other. So hang on to that letter for just a moment and watch how those two notions battle in your mind. In a flash you'll find yourself facing THREAT and being conscious of JESUS at the same time. That's the heart of this exercise.

It is putting threat and the Lord together **in your mind,** and weighing one against the other that extracts the most from this action. You can't do this in a classroom or in your chair. You have to be at the mailbox. Dropping that letter is the point of no return. So don't let go of it too quickly. Pause to consider Satan's idea ("What will he think of me?") then God's idea "Go ye" and see what happens. You'll find yourself more eager to please the Lord than Satan. Then you'll **want** to let go of the envelope. But if you hurry past this moment, routinely dropping the letter in the box, you'll miss the experience of matching threat against the Lord's presence in the critical moment.

REVIEW: I want you to get what I am saying here. We are not just talking about exercises. There's more to it than that. We are dealing with spiritual strength. It doesn't come in a flash. It develops as your awareness of the Holy Spirit increases. You find yourself more determined to please the Lord (Who is becoming increasingly real), than heed such ego-shattering thoughts as, "What will they think of me?" The more you recognize the devil as the author of your fears, the more you will discount them to delight yourself in pleasing the Lord. In my book, DEALING WITH THE DEVIL, you'll find an exhaustive treatment of how Satan puts such thoughts in our minds and what to do about it. Recognizing his working under the guise of SELF is necessary for real progress in overcoming fear.

• Plan to pay three bills. Space the actions a day apart. If you will systematically bring yourself to this exercise three times, carefully watching for Satan's suggestion (threat) and God's presence (the desire to please Him), you will catch on to the way fear is overcome. It's easier to see at this level of reduced threat. In time you will smile when you catch Satan in the process of filling your mind with the fear of what people will think. Right now, however, you have your hands full seeing how the Lord's presence works to overcome fear. It takes time to become SKILLED at it. But you will get there.

NOTE: You can see how you wouldn't want to send the same tract to the same institutions month after month. Therefore, as you establish this habit in your routine, you should vary the tracts you enclose with your bills. If you keep twelve different tracts at hand, you could send a different one each month, and then begin all over again with the start of a new year. Twelve different tracts would be enough for an effective ministry with your monthly obligations.

SECOND ASSIGNMENT

The threat increases when we come to the second action of this rung, tracts mailed to individuals. You will now have a chance to see what you have gained on the first part. If you made the gains one should make, you'll be ready. We'll find out how much you profited shortly.

In the first action you had no particular individual in mind. You mailed your tracts to institutions. You had no control over who received it. The person at the other end probably doesn't know you, unless you live in a small town where everybody knows everybody. The chances of your knowing the clerk who opens the mail in all of the utilities or institutions to which you pay bills is remote. But this time it will be different. The person who receives your tract will know it was meant for him, personally. That makes it more threatening.

There is no face-to-face contact. You continue to enjoy the safety of distance. A tract is going to do all the work for you. However, there is a sharp increase in threat when you deliberately send a gospel message to someone who knows you. They could think strange thoughts about you. You know how it is with us. We want everybody to think well of us. It could hurt if a friend suddenly judged us as a religious nut. That's the threat increase.

● A different tract is used for this action. It's called "Owe A Letter," number 404. You'll also find it in your catalog. Read it. Likely those are things you wouldn't say to a friend. But this tract is willing to do it for you when enclosed with a letter or greeting card. It has a curious punch, don't you think? Yet, as every tract should, it contains the salvation invitation.

Now let's see, is there someone you owe a letter? Most people don't write as often as they should. Maybe you are one. Does someone come to mind? Is there a relative who hasn't heard from you for a long time, or a sick friend who would appreciate a card? There are greeting cards in the stationery stores that are designed for friends who haven't written to each other in a long time. You could enclose your tract in one of those. Or, if you are reading this near some holiday, a seasonal card would be fine.

> **HINT: All you have to do is enclose the tract. You don't have to say anything about it. You need not make any reference to spiritual things at all. There is enough threat in the exercise without that. We are concerned only with your feelings as you set yourself to mail a gospel tract to someone who knows you and might wonder what you have in mind by enclosing it. That will supply all the threat we need for this rung of the ladder. If you do that and absorb the threat with some degree of comfort (as you consider the Lord) I will be satisfied with your progress.**

● Again go to the mailbox. When the letter drops from your hands this time, there will be more threat. Pause as you did in the first part of this exercise. Let the Lord's command and Satan's suggestion battle it out in your mind. Take a good look at your feelings. As you listen to Satan's idea ("What will he [she] think of me?"), you cringe a bit inside. Then as you focus on God's command ("Ye shall be witnesses unto Me") you ache to obey. Now those feelings are genuine. There is nothing artificial about this action. Once that letter slips from your hands, you can't get it back. The threat is there.

It is **talking** to the Holy Spirit that makes His presence real to you. The more you talk with anyone, the better you know him. God the Holy Spirit is no exception. Don't let anyone tell you you shouldn't speak to Him directly. He is God. To ignore Him is to ignore God. To ignore Him is to ignore Jesus. Why? The Holy Spirit is the Spirit of Christ (Acts 16:6,7 NAS). Say to Him:

"Lord God the Holy Spirit, I don't want to do Satan's will, I want to do YOUR will. Please make Yourself real to me as I prepare to send this tract in Jesus' name."

What happens to your feelings now? Take a good look at them. Sure the threat is there. You feel squeemish about doing this. Satan is busy. You don't have to do anything, you see, to develop feelings of fear. The devil sees to that. He puts the pressure on your ego. He says, "You know your friend is going to think you've gone off the deep end on religion. What will you say if he writes to you about this?"

> **NOTE:** See how you don't have to practice to develop feelings of threat? Satan does all the work for you. He can make you hesitate by putting one idea in your mind. Ah, but what did we say was needed to counteract those fears? The presence of the Spirit. Now feelings of the Spirit's presence DO NOT come automatically. You have to develop them. That's why I want you to focus on the Holy Spirit before you let go of that letter. As He makes Himself real to you, what happens to Satan's suggestion? It becomes weaker. The more real God's Spirit is to you, the less power Satan has to govern your actions. The more aware you become of the Spirit's presence, the more determined you are to please God rather than the devil. That's why this course began with the "shake test" in the locked privacy of a public restroom.

● As soon as your awareness of the Spirit's presence becomes more powerful than the threat created by the devil's suggestion, drop the letter. When it leaves your fingers the exercise is over. You will have made an important advance in conquering your fear of people. Repeat this action three times, exactly as I have described it above. By the third time you will rejoice in the fact that feelings of fear can be conquered by increased awareness of the Spirit's presence.

Learn this phrase. It captures the truth of what I have been saying here:

Christian courage is not the absence of fear. It is the

conquest of it through an awareness of the Holy Spirit's presence.

HINT: The threat in this exercise is not temporary, as in the case of leaving tracts. Satan will continually seek to bother you with thoughts such as "I wonder if he got my tract and what he thought of my sending it to him?" When those fear feelings return, let them be a signal for you to think of the Holy Spirit. Chat with Him for a brief second. Everytime this happens look on it as an opportunity to practice with the truth that an awareness of the Spirit's presence can overrule feelings of fear—if you work to develop it. Should your friend actually write to you about the tract, the only explanation I want you to give now is that you are studying this course and I told you to send the tract as an assignment. That will get you off the hook.

What happens to the tract after it leaves your hands is up to the Holy Spirit. He will have some fun with it, you can be sure of that. Your obedience in sending it allows Him to join the action with some of His own. As your acquaintance opens the letter, God's Spirit does two things: (1) He bears witness to your warm intentions, (2) He also bears witness to the truth of the message.

It's natural to think that everyone who gets a tract from you will be critical of you. That's what Satan wants you to think. He works to keep that thought alive in your mind. But the reaction of your acquaintance can just as easily be one of gratitude and appreciation when the Holy Spirit is involved. Remember: action on your part always produces action on His part. That's a spiritual law. So when someone does write back to you about the tract, it is more likely the Spirit of God has a prospect on the line.

● You will have completed the second assignment when you have written to three different people enclosing the "Owe A Letter" tract. Do it on three separate days, of course. That's to build strength.

HINT: After you have completed the 6 assigned actions for this rung of the ladder, and extracted the strengths for your own ministry, you can expand your outreach. Is there some Christian you know who should be in action for Jesus, but is doing nothing with his life but attending church? Send him a note. Tell him you are studying this course and enclose tract no. 420, "Get Wise-Witness!" You'll find it in the catalog. The Holy Spirit might use it to get him into action for Christ. If he does, you will come in for a share of all your contact produces for the Lord. This is another way to lay up for yourself "treasure in heaven" (Matt. 6:20). As soon as you have read my book, JESUS IS COMING—GET READY CHRISTIAN!, treasure in heaven will become an urgent part of your spiritual life.

● Now then, that lesson wasn't too bad, was it? You met a new threat and absorbed it. It has made you stronger. Also you have discovered a new way to reach your private world— **using the mails.** The desk where you do your writing and pay your bills can become a strategic outpost. There are many more actions I could have given you, such as putting stickers on the outside of your envelopes, and enclosing pennies with the "Penny For Your Thoughts" tract. But I will leave those for your experimentation.

I am hoping you have gained a new appreciation for reaching people via the mails and will keep your desk stocked with tracts. Once you start thinking about the possibilities of mail-witnessing, the Holy Spirit will show you all sorts of ways to use it for the Lord. He could give you some tremendous ideas for exploiting the mails for Christ. So look on this lesson as only the beginning of what you are going to do with. . . "Tracts in Letters."

HINT: As you expand your mail outreach, you will encounter those people who are not happy to find a spiritual message in their mailbox. They might even write back asking you not to send any more such items. Should this occur among any of your acquaintances, jot down the names. It might pay to start a list. If your mail outreach

expands considerably, you could collect a half-a-dozen names on that list in time.

One of our correspondence course students gave this account in her salvation letter. She said it was her task in the small office where she worked to empty the wastebaskets. For some time, one of their customers had been systematically sending a tract along with each payment. It usually landed in the wastebasket. Our student had noticed the tracts from time to time. Finally they got the best of her curiosity and she began to read them. She was saved. Today she is one of our most enthusiastic students. No one has to sell her on the way the Holy Spirit uses tracts to reach lost souls.

Who knows what is going on in a reader's heart when God's timing brings a tract to his hands? That's the FUN of working **with** the Holy Spirit. So it is not foolish to send them through the mail. The Holy Spirit has already planned on your doing it. He has people ready to receive them, people who might not be reached any other way. Therefore, "Tracts in Letters" is more than a strength-building exercise. It is an important part of your ministry to your private world. Plan on making it a permanent part.

Now you are ready for your first face-to-face contact with a prospect. Next.

Chapter Eight

PIN & TRACT

Now the real fun begins. On this 3rd step of the ladder comes your first face-to-face contact with people. But don't get scared. A tract will do all the talking for you. Yet, you will be in direct personal touch with a prospect. What is it that puts you in touch with this prospect? Ah, a provocative pin worn on your clothing.

You are about to meet the provoker concept of attracting souls. Once you see how it works, you'll be thrilled with the way it can ease you into face-to-face action. The increase in threat is gentle. You are sure to enjoy it. That's the way to make witnessing easy.

In your PC catalog, you will find tract number 413, "Since You Asked." Right after it is a question mark pin. Those are the tools needed for the "Pin & Tract" rung of the witnessing ladder. See how the question mark on the cover of the tract matches the pin? That's important. It is going to make your presentation of this tract childishly simple.

Here's how it works. Fasten the "question mark" pin on your clothing before you leave the house. As you go about, someone will spot the pin and ask, "What's the pin for?" Instead of a verbal reply, reach into your pocket and bring forth the tract, "Since You Asked," and offer it to him. When he sees the title, a smile will come to his face. He thinks it's cute. He's amused knowing his own curiosity made him bite on your pin.

Yes, this action has humor. But that's what removes the threat. You see, people can't laugh and be upset at the same time. The humor actually cancels the threat. Even so, the Lord's invitation has reached his hands. You've just presented the gospel without saying a word. And your prospect is happy about it. What could be simpler than that?

GETTING STARTED

Fasten the pin to your clothing. Fold one of the "Since You Asked" tracts and slip it into your pocket. Now go and let your wife (or some friend) observe your pin and ask about it. If you have a big grin on your face, she'll bite.

"What's the pin for, honey?"

Your smile widens. Your hand comes from your pocket with the tract. Without saying a single word, you offer her the tract. See—she smiles as she realizes the tract is your answer to her question. Right away she connects the red question mark pin on the cover of the tract with the one you're wearing. Her response will be,

"Hey, that's pretty good."

NOTE: If you are not married and no friend is at hand for this preparatory action, try it at church. Test it on one or two Christians to get the "feel" of the action. Not only will this ease you toward the more public threat of wearing the pin about your private world, it could challenge other Christians to get busy for Jesus. A typical reaction from a fellow Christian is, "Say, do you happen to have any more of those pins?" You probably will, since they come in packages of 10.

READY FOR ACTION

You've made your preparatory trial runs. Now you are ready to go on display for Christ. Before you leave the house, make sure your pin is in place and a supply of folded tracts is on your person. Pause for a chat with the Lord:

"Lord Jesus, here we go. I'm ready to work WITH you. Help me to be so aware of your presence that I will not be ashamed to wear my pin. Use me to attract anyone You wish today."

Out you go. It may be to work, or it may be an errand to the store. It doesn't matter which. What is important, is that you are now a tool of the Holy Spirit. With your provoking pin in place, you are on DISPLAY. You are available and ready with a tract should the Lord prod someone to inquire about your pin. Will you be self-conscious? Yes, but only for a little while. At first you think everyone is paying attention to your pin, but that's not so. Most will not see it. And of those that do...

Most will not say one word about it!

That's what's going to surprise you. You'll be amazed at how few will inquire. You can go for days without anyone saying a word about your pin. And then there will be days when two or three people will inquire. The look on your face has a lot to do with it. If you are glum, people will be afraid to ask. If you are cheerful and appear to be someone who is easy to approach, you will get more inquires.

Now you ask, "What's the point of wearing the pin if so few will inquire?" Ah, something is happening to you. The simple process of moving about in public as BAIT for the Holy Spirit, does have some threat. And you absorb it. You see, you never know when someone **might** ask. That keeps the threat ever present. Besides it's a new sensation for you to

106

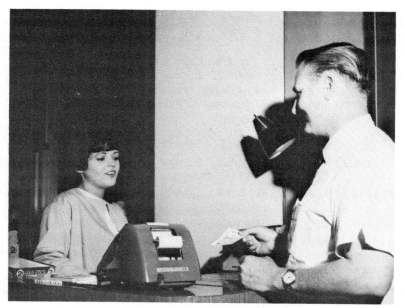

THE PIN ASKS — THE TRACT ANSWERS.

be on display for Jesus in your private world. You may not realize it, but you are being strengthened just by wearing that pin in public. Besides that, every time you fasten it to your clothes, the discipline draws your mind to Jesus.

WHEN SOMEONE ASKS

It might come as a mild shock the first time someone inquires. Why? It may have gone from your mind entirely that you were wearing the pin. The question startles you some. You may have to stop and think for a second what the inquiry means. Then it hits you, "He's seen my pin!" Now that is a bit stressful. In fact you're slightly embarrassed that you have forgotten the Lord's business—**and the Lord!** The Master sometimes allows the inquiry to come this way as a mild rebuke. But you can absorb it. You gain a little more strength as you do.

HINT: If the question catches you completely off guard and your tract isn't handy, you stall for time with a few cover words. Simply say something like this: "Oh how nice of you to notice my pin. I was hoping someone would see it and ask me about it." By that time you can get your tract out and have it ready to present. You don't need more than a second to reach to your pocket and whip out the tract with a "quick draw."

Normally, a person keeps his tracts in a holder for the purpose of maintaining their freshness and to keep the corners from bending over. Dog-eared tracts do not look very appealing. If you carry your tract holder in your shirt pocket, keep a few loose tracts between the plastic holder and your shirt pocket. That way, they are ready to be pulled from your pocket quickly without your having to remove the holder and extract the tract in a clumsy maneuver. It's embarrassing to have a prospect watch you fumble with the holder while waiting for you to dig out your printed reply to his inquiry. The tract holder will help to keep the loose tracts in nice condition, even though they are not inside the holder itself. They become pressed between the holder and the outside of your shirt pocket. (Plastic tract holder is no. 116 in catalog.)

NOTE: This "Pin and Tract" action is planned so that you do not have to say anything, not even one word. That's why at least one tract must be available at all times for the "quick draw." But that cover phrase can be useful, for sometimes silence is more embarrassing than a word or two. Therefore, familiarize yourself with the cover phrase. Why don't you tuck those words in your memory, "I'm glad you asked about my pin, etc." A situation might come along when you will need an extra second to reach for your tract.

● Your prospect accepts the tract. He looks at it. As he does, let your spirit silently talk to the Holy Spirit. Remember, we're working WITH Jesus, not just FOR Him. "Lord, bear witness to his heart," or "Use me now Lord Jesus to reach this man for You." Since this is done within your own spirit, there is nothing outward to indicate you are in communication with Christ, even as you stand before your prospect.

Now look at your man. A smile breaks across his face. He opens to the inside to discover he has just received a spiritual message. Then he chuckles. Don't let that chuckle fool you. The Holy Spirit is working. How do you know? You asked Him to. And you are in motion. He is also granting you favor at this moment. Your prospect may come back with, "What a sneaky way to get to a guy." Again, he may just think that without saying so. And then comes the signal that the Spirit is doing HIS work. The man nods his head in an affirmative gesture. He may even say something like this:

"Hey, that's pretty good. Mind if I keep this?"

Mind? Indeed not. That's why you gave it to him. The point is, the Spirit of God is giving you favor in this man's sight. I can practically guarantee you that no one will ever react with hostility to this action. The Holy Spirit uses the humor in the scene to cancel all hostility. Besides, why should anyone react negatively? Think over what really happened:

1. You were minding your own business.

2. The prospect saw your pin and he made the inquiry— curiosity.

3. You replied with a piece of paper. Even that was titled in such a way as to remind him HE was the one who asked the question.

4. He knows he is to blame for the fact that the gospel has come to his hands.

5. He is struck by the humor of the incident. He bit on your bait.

Isn't that sweet? Nearly all of the threat is removed from this presentation. As simple as it is, you haven't done too

109

badly. You have been face to face with another man. You have placed the invitation to Christ in his hands. And you have not been overly stressed by doing the action. That's nice progress, isn't it? On top of that, you have handled yourself so as to allow the Holy Spirit to participate in the operation.

My friend Jack was wearing his "Question Mark" pin while passing through the huge Farmer's Market in Los Angeles. He stopped at a small fruit stand to make a purchase. The lady waiting on him kept glancing at his pin, but didn't say a word. Yet, it was obvious she was attracted by it. Jack made his purchase, but he hadn't gone a dozen yards from the stand when this lady came running after him.

"I just have to know what that pin is for," she said, **"my curiosity has gotten the best of me?"**

Jack smiled. Without a word he brought forth the "Since You Asked" tract and gave it to her. When she saw what it was, her hand slapped the side of her face and she gave out with the self-incriminating exclamation. . .

"I goofed!"

The point? She blamed no one but herself.

When you can reach a person for Christ in such a way that he does not feel the gospel has been jammed down his throat, and he reacts toward you pleasantly, that is power—the power of know-how. When you know what you are doing, you can make your whole life an effective witness for Jesus. You will acquire such know-how as we head for the top of the ladder.

ASSIGNMENT

I want you to wear the question mark pin for at least two weeks. Make it longer if you like. It is important that you reach the place where you feel comfortable wearing such a pin in your private world. I wear one. I never leave the house without some kind of a pin on my clothing the Holy Spirit can use to attract a prospect. I feel naked without one. So stay with this action until you are comfortable. Comfort is an important word in the witnessing business. It's comfort that makes a man willing to be a witness for life.

> **NOTE: At this point in the "Pin & Tract" action we are not so concerned with the affect of your witness on the prospect. We are more concerned with YOUR feelings as you place yourself at the disposal of the Holy Spirit, than with the people who might ask about your pin. This exercise is fully successful if NO ONE inquires about it. Your strength comes from wearing the pin in public. When you become comfortable serving as BAIT for the Holy Spirit, you will have extracted the profit from this part of the action.**

NOW FOR A BIT MORE THREAT

We're going to shift pins. Replace your question mark pin with the "Ask Me" button. The latter is a bit more provocative. This time we hope someone will make an inquiry. The action, though, is the same as before. But now your attention is focused more on the prospect than on yourself and how you feel when you are face to face with him. The "Ask Me" button has a better chance of eliciting an inquiry. It's pin no. 476 in the catalog.

You are ready to leave your house once again. Your pin is in place. You have some "Since You Asked" tracts in your pocket. Before you go out, pause for a chat with the Holy Spirit. He longs to be in on everything. In fact, you have now set yourself NOT to do anything without Him.

You are on your way to the store. You check with the Spirit once again as you walk into the market. We'll suppose it is the box boy who spies your pin and comments:

"Okay, what am I supposed to ask you?"

111

This time you make a point of saying 3 or 4 words before you present the tract. I didn't require it in the first action, for I was happy to have you face to face with a prospect. But now we will inch ahead a bit further and make it a part of this exercise. You can see why, can't you? We are working our way to the place where you will be able to use your LIPS for the Lord. A wee phrase can give you a first taste. Now that the box boy has inquired about your pin, here's what I want you to say:

"I'm glad you asked."

or,

"Since you asked."

Then out comes your tract. You hand it to the boy with a smile. He smiles too. See, that wasn't too hard. Yet, you have begun speaking to a prospect in a gospel situation. For a second or two the lad studies the tract. In those same seconds, you lift your spirit to the Lord:

"Bless it to his heart, Lord."

Then watch. Remember, this time we're interested in what happens in the other fellow. The Holy Spirit will go to work, you just asked Him to. Little signs will appear about the boy's eyes and His mouth. Those signs can be read. I don't expect you to be able to interpret them now. In time, you can become quite expert in reading the external signs of the Spirit's working within a prospect. At this point, I don't want you to be expert in anything. I'm happy to have you saying those few words to your prospect as you give him the invitation to Christ. That's progress.

NOTE: Should your lad turn out to be a Christian, you haven't wasted your time. He will be challenged by your example. The Holy Spirit will cause his mind to think of the Great Commission and how you are obeying the command.

Every Christian knows he was saved to tell others, the Holy Spirit sees to that. So witnessing to a Christian can produce good results. Should the Spirit use your example to get another believer into action, it will add to your treasure in heaven.

ASSIGNMENT

Wear the "Ask Me" pin for two weeks. If you feel the responses are too slow in coming, go where the action is. Is a department store or discount house having a sale? Then go there, wearing your pin. Someone will think you are there to give assistance. And if that proves to be too slow for you, station yourself near the main entrance. Someone is bound to ask you a question like. . .

"Could you tell me where those records are that are on sale?"

The reply is natural and smooth:

"I don't work here, but I'm glad you saw my pin and asked. I do have an answer for you."

NOTE: You don't have to say any more than that. Later on, when you have developed your skill as a witness, you will be able to turn such scenes into wonderful witnessing conversations. It's very simple to add, "I think you'll find that a unique approach to the gospel." Then you pause to read the spiritual signs in the person's face. If you detect the Spirit's working, you can proceed with, "Is it possible you have some interest in spiritual things?" I mention this only to show how marvelous tracts are for creating witnessing and soul-winning interviews. Later on you'll be able to take advantage of this insight. Doesn't that encourage you to press on? Sure it does.

● As soon as the prospect accepts your tract, hastily commit him to the Lord. Ask the Spirit to use your tract. You may see the person reading the tract as he walks away from you with God's witness already speaking to his heart. It is not uncommon for a person to turn around and toss you a smile when he discovers you have given him a spiritual message. It is working WITH the Holy Spirit that makes it FUN to witness in this fashion. It is amazing how much favor HE can grant us when we trust Him for it.

> **NOTE: If you are a young person in school, you might want to try the monkey pin & tract combination. As soon as you have completed the above assignments, shift to the monkey pin. In your pocket are some of the "Monkey Business" tracts which harness the evolution controversy to the gospel. When another kid asks you about your pin, say to him, "That's my great grandfather. You've heard about the business he started, haven't you?" If the prospect says no or stares at you blankly, offer the tract. When he sees the big chimp on the cover and reads the title, "Monkey Business," it will go over big with him. For this combination, see no's. 417 and 482 in the catalog.**

For myself, I like to wear the 1¢ pin. I like the tract, "A Penny For Your Thoughts." I often bring forth a shiny penny from my pocket and give it to the inquirer so that I am actually paying a penny for his thoughts. He then feels obliged to read the tract and share his thoughts on it. It has lots of power. I've led souls to Jesus using it.

Now my wife, Margie, prefers the owl pin. She likes the "Wisest Man In The World" tract. The passing dialogue that goes with it is the easiest for her. You will want to experiment for yourself to determine which is best for you. Also it is good to change your pin and tract combinations from time to time. It adds variety to your work. Since this is an action you will want to continue for the rest of your life, variety can make it more fun for you. This type of witnessing never becomes routine when you have an arsenal of pins and techniques for provoking inquiries from your private world.

The next step will be easy now.

Chapter Nine

LIPS & TRACTS

Four weeks have gone by. You are stronger now. Wasn't it fun to make yourself a target for the Holy Spirit and let Him select prospects for you? He did most of the work. All you had to do was be ready. Even when you were face to face with the prospect, your PIN was the center of interest. It drew the attention away from you. In a sense you were hiding behind your pin. On top of that, a tract did all the talking for you. Could anything be easier?

Now you are going to come out from behind the pins. You will still wear them, of course. They won't interfere with this exercise.

No need to squirm when I speak of coming out from behind your pins. We've got to quit leaning on crutches or you won't make any progress. We'll be taking this in bites. They won't overstress you. It's vital that you learn to use your lips for Jesus. This lesson is going to acquaint you with some of the power that can be yours if you will speak out for the Lord. First let's consider the amazing privilege of communication.

COMMUNICATION

Animals can't talk. Only people can take ideas from their heads, shape them into words, and then transfer them to other minds. It is the privilege of humans to pass thoughts from one person to another by means of words. Animals have lips, but they can't say anything. But you and I, we can say things to people that may change the course of their lives. In fact, the highest force that can bear upon anyone, is the effect of someone else's words.

Not only do we have the power to plant IDEAS in other people's minds, we can also say things that will arouse their FEELINGS. Depending on the words we select, we can create almost any feeling we want in a listener. Certain words can make him feel good, others can upset him. There are words which comfort, those which produce laughter, and those which evoke love. Every human emotion can be aroused by words.

Why do we care about that? It is part of the witnessing skill to realize that IDEAS alone have little effect on people. Bare facts resting in a person's mind do little to activate him. But let those same ideas be accompanied by a powerful emotion, and they penetrate his spirit to make a lasting impression. It is going to be your privilege to learn how to present the gospel with FEELING.

● There will be three different actions on this "Lips & Tracts" rung of the ladder. Each will be a bit harder than the other. Each assignment will have a little more threat, but you need that to build witnessing muscle.

> NOTE: We have reached a critical point in the program. Our goal is to bring you to the place where you feel comfortable speaking out for Jesus. Using your lips to create a witnessing scene, which you will be doing this time, has got to be a vital point in the plan. How do you like the idea of being able to generate a witnessing situation with your lips? It means you won't have to wait any longer for people to "bite" on your pins. That's real progress, isn't it? Certainly it is an important step toward the goal of being able to speak for Christ whenever you have the opportunity. Your effectiveness rises sharply on this rung of the ladder.

FUNCTIONAL TRACTS

Don't you like the idea of being able to create a witnessing situation? Sure you do. Still, I suppose it sounds a little frightening—right? Let me set you at ease. It's going to be a lot easier than you think. Some functional tracts are going to make the action simple for you.

The functional tract is not new to you. You have already used three of them. The "Bills" tract was one designed for a **normal function** within your private world. There are always bills to pay. Was not the "Tip" tract functional also? Sure. It fitted a function quite routine for most Christians. Why, even the "Owe A Letter" tract was functional. Letter writing is also a part of your private world. What is it then that makes a tract functional? A tract is functional when it is designed to take advantage or exploit a situation that occurs regularly as you go about your routine of living. You'll see that more clearly as we come to the first action for this rung of the ladder.

Here's something you say all the time. It's hard to be around people and not say it, occasionally.

THANK YOU

How often do people say that? So often it is an automatic function of our daily lives. We do it so many times, we scarcely think about it. Yet, it can be used for Christ. You are going to learn how to exploit the common THANK YOU, and turn it into a witness for Jesus. How? By using a tract that communicates the THANK YOU for you—and harnesses it to the gospel.

In the catalog, you will find number 411 THANK YOU tract. Armed with some of these on your person, all that remains is finding a way to get one into the conversation when it is time to say "Thank you." That will be the first task for your lips in this exercise. As simple as this action may seem, it is nonetheless a high point in your witness-life. So get ready to use your lips for their most noble purpose— opening the way for someone to receive Jesus' invitation.

PICTURE THE ACTION

Some folded THANK YOU tracts are on your person. You have stopped at a coffee shop for a bite to eat. It's time to

117

pay the check. As you walk toward the cashier, you have a brief word with the Holy Spirit. You want to be aware of His presence as you do this action. The cashier accepts your money, returning your change with her "Thank you." You are all set now to give her your own. Even as your hand moves, the words come swiftly from your lips. . .

"And here's my thanks to you."

She doesn't mind being thanked. Who does? So she accepts your tract. The atmosphere is polite and cordial. There seems to be hardly any threat at all. Of course, the Holy Spirit is working. You feel His presence, she feels warmly toward you. And when she opens the tract, she will also feel His witness.

"Oh, thank you." That's the usual reaction. Now it's true that scene took but a second, yet you were, for that moment, face to face with another person inside your private world. Then—with just a few words from your lips, you created an opportunity for placing Jesus' invitation in her hands. Isn't that precious? See what can be done with a few words? The Holy Spirit really doesn't need much from us, but He does need something.

The same scene could be repeated as you sit in your car waiting for the gas station attendant to return with your credit card. A chat with the Holy Spirit prepares you. As the attendant tears off your copy of the credit slip, he will give you his thanks. If you are ready with your tract, it is a simple matter to say. . ."**And here's my thanks to you."**

NOTE: There is not the slightest bit of offense created by this type of witnessing. The THANK YOU is a common exchange among people. While saying it with a leaflet is a bit unusual, there is nothing about the scene to upset anyone. Why even the cover of the tract is designed to touch a prospect's heart. Who could get upset with a sad-eyed doggie? If people feel anything, it is pity for the poor dumb animals who can't speak. The cover of your tract does a tenderizing job on your prospect before he meets the message inside. The only reaction you will get to your THANK YOU is another, "Thank you."

I had you picture the two scenes above to show how easy it is to harness something as routine as saying thank you, to your witness-life. Granted, it takes a special tract to make it easy, but we have it.

NOTE: The action is so simple you may be tempted to think you haven't done much for Christ. Remember, it is simple because of His presence. Later on you'll be doing much harder exercises, but they too will appear simple because of your awareness of the Holy Spirit. There's no telling what HE will do with that tract or who will finally be stung by it. Once it leaves your hands it goes into circulation. That is the genius of the functional tract. Because they are so easy to use, you can get hundreds of them scattered throughout your private world. They are just marvellous for reaching people on the go.

● I told you we would begin the "Lips & Tract" action easily. Now we have started. At this point I want you to notice that it took but a few words from your lips to create the tract situation. Sure, they were simple words, but they made it possible for you to pass the tract with its invitation. Your lips turned the trick. From now on, you will be able to use this tract whenever you have an opportunity to say "Thank you."

ASSIGNMENT

I want you to do the THANK YOU action three times. Again, do not do them all in the same day. Three is all I will require. I know you will do more. As you do them, see if you can't vary the words a bit. If you can, it will help to develop your ease and poise. For example, you may find it convenient to say something like this to a clerk or someone who has waited on you:

"Your service is so good, you deserve my special thanks and here it is. . ."

That little phrase contains an element of ego-satisfaction. The person who receives it will be very pleased. And his pleasure will transfer from you to the tract he is about to read. Try it a time or two. You'll be amazed at how easy it is to say. You will also be delighted with the effect it has on the prospect. In fact, you will like what it does for your own spirit to pass such cheer on to others.

If you find you are not comfortable in the THANK YOU exercise after three times, stay with it until you are. Do not advance to the next action until you have extracted all the strength you can from sowing THANK YOU seeds throughout your private world. The next action is harder and you should make the necessary gain in comfort before going to it.

I FEEL GREAT

Now we come to another automatic function within your private world—saying "Hello" to people. We're going to harness the common greating of, "Hi, how are you today?" And we're going to do it with a tract. In the catalog, you'll find no. 422. . ."I FEEL GREAT!"

Let's visualize the action.

You've picked up a couple of items at the store. They are in your shopping cart as you head for the checkout stand. You have been here often enough to know the cashier usually says, "How are you today?" This time you are going to take advantage of that situation. You are going to exploit it for Christ with the tract you just read.

120

You chat with the Holy Spirit as you roll toward the cashier:

"Lord, this action is going to be harder for me. Please help me to be aware of your presence."

The clerk greets you with the expected. . ."How are you today?" Now it's your turn. Let the words come out with enthusiasm:

"I feel great! Really great!" (Pause—as you offer the tract). **But you'll have to read this to find out why!"**

As soon as the cashier sees the title of your tract, "I Feel Great!" his face breaks into a smile. He'll stop long enough to examine it to see what he has just received. As soon as he discovers it is a tract, his reply will be "Thanks, I'll read it later." Then it will either go into his pocket or on a shelf near his cash register.

Of course you could have given him a THANK YOU tract as you were leaving, and it would have been a lot easier. But we are deliberately increasing the threat this time.

NOTE: Not only have we increased the threat, but we now add a new ingredient to your witness—enthusiasm. It is not too early in the course for you to think of your personality as a tool. It can be sharpened and used for the Lord. Did you know that enthusiasm is infectious? You bet it is. It is highly contagious. People respond to enthusiasm in others. If you enrolled in a sales course from any of the success schools about the land, one of the first things they'd build into you is enthusiasm. It works like magic. It is the secret of success in selling. It adds fantastic power in witnessing.

 Once there was a salesman who called on farmers to acquaint them with a newly developed cream separator. He was so sold on his product, he didn't believe a farmer could refuse to buy it, if he knew what it would do for him. This, of course, made him very enthusiastic in his presentations. He put his whole heart into every demonstration. In fact, he loved to demonstrate what the new machine would do.

One day he called on a farmer who had a good reason for refusing to buy a new separator. "I have only one cow," he said, "I don't need a separator." But the salesman persuaded him to let him give the demonstration in case he got more cows later on. Excitedly he proceeded with his sales pitch. You could tell he was thrilled with his product. He loved talking about it, and it showed. In fact, his enthusiasm was so great and so catching, this farmer not only bought one of the separators, he traded in his only cow for the down payment.

Now that was powerful selling.

A funny story? Sure. Yet, it illustrates the power of enthusiasm. It is contagious and it moves people. If you will make a point of adding this ingredient to your witnessing, your success will rise higher and higher. People love others who are enthusiastic. They like to be around them. So don't be afraid to add a little gusto to your action. Be enthusiastic. It will do wonders for your personality and give you a great deal of power with people. Then you will have something really great to give the Holy Spirit. Now let's see how this action adds more threat.

MORE THREAT?

Yes. Your tract is presented to the cashier at the BEGIN-NING of the conversation. This means you have to stand there facing him while he rings up your groceries and sacks them for you. That is added stress. But it is not so much that you can't handle it. After all, there was humor in the incident. Just enough to cancel any critical feelings a clerk might otherwise have.

However, he knows you are some sort of a religious person. You are identified with the tract. If he read enough of it. to spot the words, "Jesus Christ is the only way to God," he also knows you are a Christian. The Holy Spirit will even tell him you belong to Jesus. Can you stand that? I mean, can you bring yourself to stand there facing a person who knows you are agressive for Christ? I hope you can.

HINT: A clerk who is a little slow catching on to things might accept the tract from your hand, but follow with an inquiry. He might look at it, and then ask, "What is this?" It doesn't happen very often, but should it, I want you prepared. Your instant reply would be. . ."Something that could make you feel great too!" That doesn't give away any information, yet it will satisfy the clerk. You could add, if you have the nerve, "Read it and find out. I think you will be pleasantly surprised." Such words could add to his curiosity.

Other places

There are other places where this action can be carried out. Bank tellers usually ask this question, so do receptionists in doctor's offices. If you meet the mailman in the yard or at the door, he could ask it too. Salesmen make a point of it. Whether you are at the gas station or a ticket counter, people usually ask, "How are you today."

But what if they don't?

That's easy, you ask them.

Let's see how that works

You're coming out of the discount center. The security guard stands by the exit leading to the parking lot. He eyes you as you're about to leave the store. He's too interested in your packages to say anything to you. So you flash him a smile and start the action yourself:

"How are you?"

"Fine." That's the usual reply.

"Me too. In fact I really feel great! Here, read this, it will tell you why!" The greater your enthusiasm, the greater his curiosity.

ASSIGNMENT

From what we've said so far, you can see how this could be used almost anyplace in your routine. It's hard to leave the house without running into someone who will greet you. Even if they don't, I want you to initiate an action. It won't hurt you to be the one to say, "How are you today?"

> HINT: Should you find yourself in a situation where you cannot get your tract out fast enough, use a stalling line to gain an extra second. Suppose the clerk says, "How are you today?"—Oops, your tract wasn't as handy as you thought. Then insert the stalling phrase, "Say, it was nice of you to ask me that. You know, to tell you the truth (now you have your tract). . .I feel great! Just great! And this will tell you why!"

Armed with that much insight, I want you to do this exercise five times. But not five times in a row. Space your actions over five separate outings. That way you not only get used to threat, it also gears your mind to the witnessing habit. You'll have to purpose five occasions. That will do much to establish the discipline in you.

Five times is a ridiculous assignment. I should have said 20 or even 30. But I will be happy if you do it five times. That way we don't bog down and you keep moving through the course.

> NOTE: Think of the contacts you can make for Christ now that you have the THANK YOU and HOW ARE YOU areas harnessed to the gospel invitation. Equipped with those two expressions, you can just about reach anyone you want to

within your private world. You hear these common exchanges between people everywhere. The functional tract makes it possible for you to exploit all of them for Christ.

The more you do this action WITH the Holy Spirit, the more HE will prepare you for the next action. It is going to be a lot harder. You will be working with a very powerful emotion. Therefore, I would like you to feel as relaxed as possible with the "Lips and Tract" technique, before attempting what I am about to describe. Your mind should be somewhat free of mechanics. That will allow you to concentrate on the emotion generated by the next action.

WOULD YOU BE EMBARRASSED?

That's not a question I am asking of you, but the title of the tract designed for the next action. You'll find it is no. 407 in the catalog. It harnesses one of the most powerful of human emotions—embarrassment. The truths of this tract are potent by themselves, but when clothed with this mighty emotion, they are driven home with terrific force! This is an action the Holy Spirit can use with startling effect.

The technique calls for you to produce a slight bit of embarrassment in your prospect before you present the tract. His feelings will then attach themselves to the truths to give them greater impact. In the last action it was YOUR emotion (enthusiasm) that gave force to the tract. Now it is the PROSPECT'S emotion that is going to be used. You are being exposed to this powerful technique here. Later, in Chapter Thirteen, you will be using it more precisely.

As soon as you complete this action, you will be aware of an increased boldness. If you do the assignment WITH the Holy Spirit, you will develop some real witnessing muscle.

Let's watch the action

Your work day has ended. You are leaving the job. You notice another employee whose car is parked beside yours in the parking lot. He seems to be looking for something in the trunk of his car. It would be most natural for you to speak to him, if only to say goodnight. But then it occurs to you to speak to the Lord first:

"Lord Jesus, by any chance are you detaining this man that I might witness to him? If so, I'm willing. Help me to be aware of your presence and I will try the 'embarrassed' action."

The other employee is apparently in no hurry. There's time for some small talk. No one else is close by. The two of you are quite alone, standing at the rear of his car. The conversation is friendly. But you know what you and the Lord have purposed to do. At a convenient break in the conversation, you ask him. . .

"Do you mind if I ask you a personal question?"

"No, I guess not."

"Do you get embarrassed easily?"

"Naw, not me."

"Then this is just for you."

With that you offer the tract. He'll smile a bit when he reads the title. He may think it is a dirty story. Your question hasn't embarrassed him a bit, but when he finds he has been handed a gospel tract, he could suffer a little. If he has been using a little profanity and making off color statements, he will feel a little red under the collar. That's great. The more embarrassed he is, the better. The witness will be that much more powerful when he reads the tract. His feelings will add to the truth.

126

Should your prospect ask, "What's this?" Your instant reply would be:

"It's for people who don't get embarrassed easily."

"Oh? Thanks, I'll read it."

"I hope you do, it could save you a great deal of embarrassment some day."

See? That isn't too hard. Of course, it is a lot easier for a man to ask that question of another man. The emotional content rises when a man asks a woman, "Do you get embarrassed easily?" Not knowing what to expect, and thinking an off-color joke might be coming, women suffer genuine embarrassment when asked that question. The same is true, to a lesser degree, when a woman asks the same question of a man.

• At this point, a reader might ask two questions: (1) Is it proper for a man to ask such a question of a woman in a public place? (2) Why does asking people if they get embarrassed easily, produce feelings of embarrassment in some folks?

First, it is perfectly proper for a witness to ask someone of the opposite sex if they get embarrassed easily. When you say, "May I ask you a personal question?" you have, in effect, secured the prospect's permission. That is what makes it proper. A man need not hesitate to ask this of a woman, or vice versa.

Secondly, the mere asking if people get embarrassed easily, triggers that emotion in some people. Why? It causes their minds to go back to an embarrassing event in the past. When that happens, some of the former embarrassment is resurrected. The prospect begins to relive some of those awful feelings. Those relived feelings are what you want. As soon as the tract goes into his hands, the prospect's feelings attach themselves to it. They then become emotional clothing for the truths.

HINT: Since this approach has the power to generate embarrassment, it is a good idea to practice the dialogue at home before trying it on a prospect. If there is no other Christian around who shares your witnessing ambitions, use your mirror. The fellow in there is a good friend of yours. He'll understand. You might feel a little foolish doing this before a mirror, but do it anyway. It will help the words to come from your lips AUTOMATICALLY. You are now reaching the place where you should be concentrating less and less on what you are saying, and more and more on what the Spirit is doing. Every skill takes practice, so devote some to witnessing. It is definitely a skill.

EASING INTO ACTION

See where the force of this approach lies? It's in the word, "PERSONAL." It is saying, "May I ask you a **personal** question?" that triggers feelings within the prospect. If you merely say, "May I ask you a question," you simply appeal to the ego and it is not nearly so effective. I understand this new threat, so I am going to suggest a way to try the action with a less threatening approach. Of course, reducing the threat also reduces the power. But you understand that.

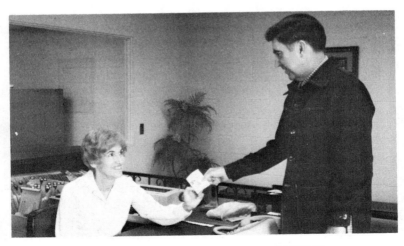

YOU START' — THE TRACT FINISHES.

128

We'll suppose you are a woman this time, and a man has just waited on you in the store. He has given you courteous service. Even as he was assisting you, there was time for a chat with the Holy Spirit. "Is this someone WE could reach with the 'Embarrassed' tract, dear Lord? Your hand busily gets the tract ready for a quick draw. With your business with the clerk about over, you speak:

"You have been very nice to help me. Would it embarrass you if I said. . .

. . .you have a nice way of dealing with people?
. . .I like your manner very much?
. . .I appreciate your sweet smile?
. . .I admire that jacket you are wearing?
. . .etc.

Any one of those or anything similar would do fine. The point is to introduce the word EMBARRASSED into the conversation.

"Oh, no. It wouldn't embarrass me."

"Good. Then I'm sure you will appreciate this." (Offer tract.)

"What's this?"

"It's something for people who don't get embarrassed easily."

NOTE: You can see how it would be possible to develop a host of ways to use this tract. All you have to do is get the word "Embarrassed" into the conversation, then offer the tract, explaining it is for people who don't get embarrassed easily. Should your prospect be of another mind and say, "Yes, I do get embarrassed," then turn your reply around and say, "This is for people who get embarrassed easily." It works just as well either way, and you don't have to be flustered should you get an answer different from what you expected.

ASSIGNMENT

Do this action three times. It may sound easy on paper, but it really isn't. This is a difficult assignment. But it won't hurt you to force yourself to do it. A marvellous strength will rise within you if you can do it. If, after the three times, you feel you never want to use it again, that is okay with me. It is also fine with me, if you would like to use the EASIER dialogue for the first one of the three. But make sure that at least two of them carry the full force of, "Mind if I ask you a **personal** question?"

Stay alert to the Holy Spirit's part. Do not allow yourself to be so occupied with your own feelings and words, that you miss what God's Spirit does with the EMOTION generated by your approach. It is powerful and you need to see the power of it. It will be good for you to experience the raw POWER at work when you give the Holy Spirit something like this to use. If you are not too desperate to get the action over with, you will be able to SEE Him at work in this situation.

The moment the tract leaves your hands, speak to the Holy Spirit:

"Lord, use this for Your glory and let me see Your power at work!"

HINT: Are you wondering what that prospect will say next time he sees you in his store? Don't give it a thought. He will not say one word—unless the Spirit prods him to. And should he speak to you about it, it will come out like this: "Say, I read what you gave me and it was pretty good." That's all. You could return to the very same place and deal with the same man an hour later and the subject will never come up. How come? Unless that clerk is a Christian, the whole matter is too painful to mention. The unsaved would rather forget it, than say anything if your tract did not find favor in their hearts. So don't be afraid to make this type of witness in a place where you shop regularly.

RELAX

I've given you your assignment. We could stop right here. But I want to make a suggestion which could add to your strength. Work with this action until you can do it RELAXED. Why? Then you'll be able to watch the Holy Spirit. It will develop your power as a witness if you would be willing to do that. You see, it is a fantastic thing to be able to stir an emotion in a prospect and at the same time present him with a tract that is based on that same emotion.

Relaxation allows you to talk with the Spirit. When you relax, HE is able to do His best work. Why? You're not trying to do it. You feel no stress one way or the other. The Spirit of God is carrying the ball, not you. I want you to come to the place where you are somewhat nonchalant as you do your part. When you reach that point, you can look for and see amazing things occur before your eyes.

Let's assume you are relaxed as you present the embarrassed tract. You have forgotten yourself. You are almost like a spectator watching the Spirit in action.

Look at your prospect's face. Lines appear on his cheeks. His lips twitch slightly. His face registers change as he reacts to the working of the Spirit. You can read him. His face tells you what is going on inside. You are not worried about your technique or what the prospect might think of you. That's great. It means you will be able to SEE the Spirit's working. It is being able to forget yourself for a moment that allows you to behold God's power before your eyes.

Once this happens, you'll hunger for more. Working in God's power is an unforgettable experience. Yet, it is one which comes only as you learn to RELAX and trust the Spirit to do His part. The correct attitude is, "I have the easy part in making the presentation, the Holy Spirit will do the hard part inside the prospect." Then set yourself to watch Him do it.

HINT: If you can put your confidence in the Holy Spirit as I've just outlined, He will not only use your witness, He will also give you FAVOR in the sight of your prospect. Your man will have the awareness of dealing with God, not you. You are in the background, so to speak. His encounter is with the truth of God as certified by the Spirit. If you will work on this aspect of the "Lips & Tract" technique, your boldness and poise will soar. No, you can't get it by reading this book. It comes by experience only. I am hoping that many of you will want to stretch yourselves as far as you can with this exercise. The rewards in your spirit are fantastic.

REVIEW

Note the ground we have covered in this step.

1. You began by using your lips to create a tract-passing situation at the END of the conversation. You said just enough words to make it possible to offer the "Thank You" tract.

2. Then you said some words at the BEGINNING of the conversation which exploited the common greeting, "How are you today?" You harnessed it to the "I Feel Great!" tract. With this witness you used YOUR enthusiasm (an emotion) to generate curiosity in your prospect. You gained some strength by continuing to face this prospect until your dealings with him were concluded. The focus was on **your** feelings.

3. In the 3rd action you deliberately sought to trigger embarrassment in your prospect, which would then be exploited by the tract, "Would You Be Embarrassed?" The power of the gospel was multiplied as the truths of your tract became clothed with his feelings of embarrassment. As soon as you reach the place where you can SEE the Holy Spirit use your work in power, your boldness rises sharply.

Well now, do you feel like you've really been through something? You might. You've come quite a way. As you look back down the ladder, you can see the rungs you've climbed so far:

1. After getting acquainted with the Holy Spirit in the action world, you began leaving tracts in secret. In time you found you could be a little more open about it. However, you made it your business to move carefully as an agent for Christ in your private world.

2. Then you started using the mails. You found that here was a vast untapped region that could be exploited for Christ by the steadfast use of tracts in all of your mailings.

3. Next you ventured into the open, wearing a pin the Holy Spirit could use to attract inquirers. You didn't have to say anything, if you didn't want to. Yet the action brought you face to face with prospects in your private world. A special tract, "Since You Asked," made it possible for you to present the gospel challenge without saying one word.

4. Now you have come to the place where you don't have to wait for people to seek you out and ask you about your pins. You can use your lips to create a witnessing situation almost any time you are around people. With just a few words you can create your own witnessing opportunities to press the Lord's invitation into people's hands. You also know something of how feelings can reinforce the message of your tract.

Yes, indeed, you've come quite a way. If you stopped right here, and went no further up the ladder, I'd feel gratified. At least you have the means for reaching your private world, and that's more than most Christians have today. I know you are not ready to rest on your laurels just yet, but isn't it comforting to know you can do the job Jesus gave you? You bet it is.

Whether you realize it or not, you've changed. You are not the same person who started this course some weeks ago. Your confidence is greater. Your awareness of the Holy Spirit and His part in doing MOST of the work has lifted a big burden from you. You also have some nice skill for reaching your private world. Don't you wish other Christians could have what you have? Of course you do.

Now that you are fairly well equipped as a witness for Christ, you've got something choice to share with other Christians. So let's take "Time Out For Testimony." That's next.

Chapter Ten

TIME OUT FOR TESTIMONY

After your steady advance up the ladder through rung number four, I suppose "Time Out For Testimony" sounds pretty good. No doubt you feel you need a breather. You do, but you won't be idle. You are still going to be in action. The breather comes as the result of not having to learn anything new this time.

In the past weeks you have been working with the Holy Spirit, learning different ways to reach your private world. You've come to the place where you can use your lips to create a tract situation. That's a long way from where you were when we started out. That means you have something worth sharing. With whom? Your brethren, particularly those confined to the world of theory. You are now in a position to challenge and help those whose spiritual energies are limited to church routines.

NOTE: Whenever a Christian comes across something that helps him to live for Christ and joyously serve Him, he has an obligation to share it with the brethren. There are those Christians who have faced the fact that the Lord has more for them than they are getting in churchianity. They feel they are coming short of the abundant life the Lord promised. These are the ones toward whom you have an obligation. Even though they sense there is more to the Christian life than a few meetings each week, there is no one to rescue them unless people like you come to their aid. Because your own life is sampling the thrill of Christ, you can infect others. The witnessing bug is contagious.

ACTION

Go to prayer-meeting. Be prepared to do four things:

1. Request prayer support for your personal ministry.
2. Explain to the brethren why you need it.

3. Challenge them to reach their private worlds.
4. Be on the lookout for a prayer-partner.

Does your church have weekly prayer-meetings? Does it provide for testimonies from the various ones? Good. Be ready to get to your feet. Don't attempt to be professional. Even though you are before Christians, the Holy Spirit must still do 90% of the work. There is nothing you can do without Him, whether ministering to an unsaved prospect or your brethren. So relax. Don't worry about mistakes or clumsiness. Let Him have your simplicity and informality. Most of all, present a gentle, non-critical attitude.

> **CAUTION:** A haughty or judgmental attitude will make you powerless in the Spirit. It is easy for those who are busily reaching their private worlds for Christ, to be critical of those who limit their spiritual activity to church functions. God is not pleased when a Christian behaves as though he has something his brothers do not. You've seen this attitude in other Christians who felt they were gifted in some way and know how spiteful and divisive it is. It is just as ugly for a witness to behave this way. So keep yourself low and the Holy Spirit will use you. You'll be amazed at the results of your work if your presentation is truly humble.

If your church does not provide for testimonies in the prayer-meeting, then you can do this action just as well in a Sunday school class or any Christian group that allows the brethren to share what the Lord does in their lives. However, it should be a group with which you meet regularly. Otherwise, it would not be a part of your normal routine. Now should your church have a prayer-meeting that encourages testimonies, and you haven't been attending, plan to get started. Maybe you haven't felt the need before, but now you will. God has a way of reinforcing His people when they meet together to serve Him in prayer.

> **HINT:** If you attend the church's regular prayer-meeting, check with the pastor ahead of time. Explain that you'd

like a few minutes to tell about your witnessing and ask for prayer support. If he consents happily, the door is open for you. If he appears reluctant, then the prayer-meeting may not be the right place for your testimony. What you are going to do could take as long as ten minutes, if you are inept in your presentation, less if you are smooth. You don't want the pastor displaying anguish over the time you are using, it could kill the spirit of the meeting. If you get his OK first, there should be no problem.

● When you are recognized, let your first words be the request for prayer:

"I need your help in prayer, dear brethren. The Lord has led me to take a good look at the Great Commission and has challenged me to obey it. I knew I couldn't go into ALL the world, so when I asked the Lord about it, He showed me the only world I could reach is my own private world."

"Perhaps some of you have never heard of the believer's private world. I hadn't either until recently. For that reason I have brought along a crude sketch. It will show you what my private world looks like. When you see what I am trying to do for the Lord, you'll understand why I need your help in prayer."

From your pocket take out a large sheet of folded paper. You may even wish to prepare a cardboard chart. When opened, your private world looks very much like the drawing on page 39 of this text. Your own world will vary in places, but it will still have the round, world-like shape. It will show the scope of your outreach for Christ.

"All of us have private worlds. Mine looks like this. Yours may look a little different, but essentially they have one thing in common. They include the people we can reach in the course of our daily routine."

NOTE: I won't spell out all you could say about your private world. You can draw on the material in the early chapters of your text, sharing the highlights with the group. But make it brief. The most important point is that each person has a private world. And within that world are people he can reach better than anyone else. The Great Commission makes him a missionary to that world. It will be a shock for them to consider that a change in location (per the foreign missionary) does not change one's responsibility. No matter where a man lives he has a private world and God expects him to reach it.

"Now that you have seen what I am trying to do, would you be interested in how the Lord is leading me to go about it? It really is exciting."

Nodding heads will advise you of the group's interest. Glance toward the pastor or the leader of the group to see if he approves. If he does, then turn to the person next to you and coax him into a response:

"Do you see this pin I am wearing?" (The question mark pin).

"Yes."

"Ask me about it. Say anything you like."

"Okay. What's the pin for?" (The usual reply).

Your hand comes swiftly from your pocket and offers him the tract, "Since You Asked." The group watches in rapt silence. This action is fascinating. The man accepts the tract. When he spies the title, he breaks into a smile. Coax him once again, "Tell the folks the title of the tract." When he does, the group will be impressed. Explain how a person can make this kind of a witness without saying one word.

Now turn to the person on the other side of you. Coax him:

"Ask me how I feel."

"All right, how are you?"

"I feel great! Just great! But you'll have to read this to find out why!" Again your hand moves swiftly to bring forth the tract.

The group will laugh at your explosive enthusiasm. But it will laugh even more when the person who received the tract displays the title..."I Feel Great!" Don't stop to comment on the functional tract. Keep moving so that you do not drain away the pastor's time.

"This time I'm going to ask someone in this room a question. When I do, it will create a situation that will allow me to present a tract. Whenever I can ask this question, I can witness. Now watch closely."

Using the element of surprise, walk over to someone a few chairs away. Looking directly at him (or her) say:

"May I ask you a personal question?"

"Yes, I guess so."

"Do you get embarrassed easily?"

"Sometimes."

139

"Then this is just for you. It's for people who sometimes get embarrassed."

The people will chuckle. This time they were expecting you to come up with a tract that fitted the situation. When the "prospect" shares with them the title, "Would You Be Embarrassed?" the folks will give out with enthusiastic approval. If you have kept yourself low, the Holy Spirit will give you wonderful favor in their sight. Most of them have already begun thinking to themselves, "You know, I believe I could do that."

Exploit what you've done.

"I've shown you three of the techniques the Lord has been teaching me. There are lots more. I'm still learning, in fact I have five more steps to go before I finish the course I'm taking. But with what I have learned so far, I am able to put the invitation of Christ into the hands of nearly every person I talk to."

"It's thrilling to use know-how like this, but it is powerless without the Holy Spirit's ministry. That's why I need your prayer support. I have two specific requests to make of those of you who would be willing to pray for me. First, that I will lean more fully on the Holy Spirit and not attempt anything in my own strength. Secondly, that I will be able to move on up the more advanced steps."

"I'm very serious about this. Would any of you be willing to remember me and my two requests?"

● Some hands will go up. That, of course, challenges still more to raise their hands. Nod your appreciation and voice your thanks. Then, reach into your pocket and bring out a prayer card and a pen. Look toward the pastor. "Would it be okay, pastor, if I took just a second to get these names? So that it won't be a one-way street, I need the names so that I can remember to pray for them."

NOTE: If the group is small, say about a dozen people, you will probably be able to do this on the spot. If the group is larger than that, then ask the interested ones to see you after the meeting. Should the entire group consent to pray for you, ask the pastor if it would be all right for you to pass the sheet around for signatures. You can see how a feeling of commitment goes with signing one's name. People often promise to pray, but never think of it again. This technique will reinforce the seriousness of your request. Some will even feel guilty should they fail to remember you to the Lord.

OBSERVE

What you said about a person reaching his private world, your dramatic presentations followed by your urgent request for prayer, have brought a new seriousness to witnessing. You mean business for Jesus and it shows. What a challenge this is to the group. Practical demonstrations are always startling. They shatter the theory world. Those seeing you in action at this meeting, and feeling the impress of your anointed challenge, will be moved to follow your example. At the very least they will be asking themselves, "What's to keep me from witnessing like that?"

NOTE: There's an unmatched eloquence in what you have just done before this prayer-meeting group. Each person present couldn't help but see and feel the possibilities for reaching his own private world. Without any kind of scolding, without even a hint of criticism, you have challenged them to their shoe tops. Even as you did this, your attitude was one of thankfulness to the Lord for salvaging you from silence. In no way did you lord it over your listeners. That is what will make it easy for them to receive the truth from you.

● While that prayer card (or a sheet of paper) is being circulated, you will have time to extract some more profit from this meeting. Out of your pocket comes a copy of WITNESSING MADE EASY. You hold it up for all to see. After all, wouldn't it be cruel to bait them with your demonstrations and then fail to tell them how they can secure the skill for themselves?

> "If some of you are wondering how you might get started reaching your private worlds, I'll be glad to let you look at my copy of WITNESSING MADE EASY. Everything I have demonstrated is right here in detail. After you see it, some of you might want to get copies of your own."

(Set the book aside. Prepare for another pin & tract action).

> "Now watch what I am doing. . ."

The group watches while you remove your question mark pin and replace it with an OWL pin. It's no. 478 in your catalog. With the new pin in place, ask this question:

> "How many would like to know what this OWL pin is for?"

Hands will go up. Your next action depends on the size of the group. If the crowd is larger than 20 people, say to them. . .

> "See me after we're dismissed, and I'll give you the surprise that goes with it."

If the crowd is no larger than a dozen people, reach into your pocket and pull out a handful of "Get Wise. . .Witness" tracts. You don't have to say anything. Merely walk around the room, giving a tract to each person who raised his hand. Likely any who didn't raise his hand will want one also. Curiosity is a great motivator. There will be some chuckles when they connect the "Get Wise" with the owl.

NOTE: No one will throw the tract away. It can do a job for you. The brethren will associate its message with your demonstrations. That way you don't have to take any more time from the meeting. It will tell them about the ladder-method of witnessing and add a nice touch to your presentation. It could even produce some results for you. Every Christian you ease into the witness-life enhances your own reward at the Judgment Seat of Christ.

SIT DOWN

With that, be seated. Remain silent for the rest of the meeting. If your pastor is sensitive to the leading of the Spirit, he may feel the Lord has brought something remarkable to this meeting. It is no small thing to have someone demonstrate how EVERY Christian could witness for Christ—if he wanted to. Should the pastor be so impressed by the Spirit, he may set aside whatever else was planned and open the meeting for questions.

What you have learned so far will enable you to answer a lot of questions. However, some are sure to ask questions that pertain to lessons which are still ahead of you. If you are asked something that is apparently beyond your present stage, don't hesitate to say, "I don't know yet. Ask me that when I've finished the course."

HINT: If you are one of my students, enrolled in the correspondence course, then you will have some application blanks on your person. The Lord might use you to involve some others. There could be some who would like to ascend the ladder with me as their coach. If you are not

one of my students, then it would be a good idea to have one of the PC catalogs on your person. Some will be interested in the tools available from PC. Perhaps the pastor will show the most interest. Mention that PC is happy to send information and catalogs to anyone who writes in.

On the other hand, should the pastor take over and proceed with his meeting in the usual way, be content with what God has allowed you to do. Do not appear pushy in any way. After the meeting is over, make yourself available to any who might come to you. It may surprise you to see that several are genuinely interested in reaching their private worlds. Often you can do your best work when someone comes to you privately.

If a person comes to you who appears to be very shy, that is someone you should encourage. Shy people frequently ache to serve Jesus, but their shyness keeps them inactive. These are the ones you can help most. Having gone through the first four steps, you know how this plan reaches down to the shiest Christian and gently lifts him one step at a time. If you are shy, yourself, then you can assuredly testify what it has done for you.

PRAYER-PARTNER

In nearly every group of praying Christians, the Holy Spirit has people He is prodding toward active duty as witnesses. As you share your ministry with the brethren, see if you can't discipline yourself to read some of the faces. See if you can't find someone displaying an unusual interest. As you look at that person over a period of time, see if the Lord grants you an inner witness concerning him. If he comes up to you after the meeting is over, that will be another clue. This could be a possible partner for you.

NOTE: Before you went to this meeting, you asked the Holy Spirit about this very thing. If He has someone

144

present who might be willing to share the witness-life with you, he (she) could be a great blessing to you. So, when the different ones come to you after the meeting, check silently with the Spirit. Ask Him if this person or that person is someone He has selected as a prayer-partner. It would be great if your partner could come from this group. That way you would be assured of seeing each other often. The key indicators will be his interest in witnessing and your reaction to his personality. God would not team you with someone whose personality clashed with yours.

Please take the matter of a partner seriously. Two people working together provide great encouragement for each other. The idea of another pair of eyes watching your obedience introduces a holy discipline. Do not look to your wife or husband, or anyone of the opposite sex. I don't need to say why, do I? With a partner checking on your faithfulness, you will find you don't slack off so easily. His eyes become the eyes of the Lord. On those occasions when you have a chance to witness together, you'll find your boldness doubled and tripled.

WHAT IF YOU'RE NOT THE FIRST?

By that I mean, what if others have given these same demonstrations before you? It's possible that various ones in your church discovered the ladder-method of witnessing and have already given these demonstrations to the prayer group. What then? Can you go ahead with the step as outlined above? Indeed. But you will have to make some slight variations. For the most part you can do all of the action, including the demonstrations.

NOTE: Of course, you could go to other groups within the church such as the Sunday school classes and the ladies or men's fellowship meetings. That is an obvious alternative. But it really isn't necessary. Besides, I'm sure you prefer to make your presentation at the regular prayer-meeting. Usually the pillars of the church are there, and you stand a good chance of stirring them to action. Also, you want the backing of the church's prayer-warriors and you find them at the prayer-meeting.

By making the slight adjustments which I will show you now, you can go before the prayer-meeting group and make your presentation, even though someone else has given the same demonstrations not too long before.

Your opening remark would be altered to say:

> "Some weeks (maybe days) ago, brother (so and so) stood here and asked for your prayer support. Well, it's my turn now. I too am trying to reach my private world for Christ. Mine looks a little differently than his. . .(and then bring forth your own chart)."

> NOTE: It's not likely that any two will have exactly the same daily routine, therefore, the charts will have some variation. Did you pick up the phrase, "It's my turn now?" Remember that. That's what allows you to come along right after someone else. Twenty people could do this on successive prayer-meeting nights, and it would not be dull at all. Actually, the Holy Spirit would use the repetition to penetrate the stubborn hearts of those refusing to reach their private worlds for Christ. So don't feel bad if someone has already given a presentation to your church ahead of you. Just keep in mind, "It's my turn now," and you can go through the same demonstrations with the variations I'm showing you here.

Then you continue:

> "I suppose you've also noticed that I am wearing the same type of pin. Who's going to ask me about it?" (Nod your head toward someone. He'll respond and you can demonstrate the pin and tract action.)

As soon as you complete the Pin & Tract action, proceed immediately with the next action:

> "Now who's going to ask how I feel?"

If there is no immediate response, look toward an eager face and say, "You?" The person will pick up the cue and ask how you feel. That will allow you to go through the "I Feel Great!" routine and pass your tract.

Put your own brand of enthusiasm into the "I feel great!" That is what will make your presentation different from any that might have gone before you. As soon as you have presented the tract, move on to the next action:

"Now let's see. . .whom shall I pick on to embarrass?"

The people will chuckle. They know what's coming. Make your selection and walk toward that person. It is possible that your victim will come out with a bold. . ."Naw, not me. I never get embarrassed." In that case you would produce a big smile and reply:

"Then this is just for you. It's for people who never get embarrassed."

NOTE: If the folks remember the scene from the last time this technique was demonstrated, they will get a big bang out of the flexibility of the approach. It doesn't matter what a prospect says, you can always come back with the reply that the tract is for those who don't (or do) get embarrassed easily. Even if this action has been demonstrated to this same crowd fifty times, the listeners will still appreciate the novelty. Besides, each time it is presented the personality of the witness is different. It seems new each time. No two people demonstrate the techniques exactly alike. After a time, the group becomes interested in seeing how the different ones will make their presentations.

Exploiting what you've done

"I don't know how many of you responded to (so and so's) offer to explain the 'Ladder-method' of witnessing. But I would be glad to let any of you who are interested take a

147

look at my manual after prayer-meeting. Then I could explain to you how it works."

For a brief moment hold up your copy of WITNESSING MADE EASY. They've seen it before. Likely, however, only a few were interested enough to inquire. Perhaps, now that you have made your presentation, accented by your own personality touches, more people will be interested in checking with you after the meeting is over.

While the people watch, reach into your pocket and fasten the OWL pin to your dress or lapel. You are going to use it for the final challenge:

"Are there any here who have never seen an OWL pin like this, and would like to know how it is used?"

If it has been some time since the group has witnessed a presentation, there could be new people present who have never seen these skills demonstrated. Also, there might be visitors. It would be good to infect them with the witnessing virus. Beyond these, there might even be members of the church who haven't been to prayer-meeting for some time, and they just happened to be present on the night you took "Time Out For Testimony." Any of these people would be fine candidates for your "Get Wise—Witness" tract.

NOTE: Do you see how this slight altering of the presentation allows you to demonstrate the techniques and seek prayer support no matter how many times the ladder-method has been displayed before? The repetition, instead of being a hindrance, can be used by the Holy Spirit to stir some of the more sluggish ones. For a group to see one man after another rise to his feet and announce that he is working with the Holy Spirit to reach his private world, is bound to have an effect on the inactive ones. In time, more and more members of your church will be going into action. So don't hesitate to go before the prayer-meeting crowd no matter how many times they have seen the demonstrations before.

So here's what can happen when you take "Time Out For Testimony."

1. **You stir others to action.**
2. **You win prayer support for your ministry.**
3. **You could locate a possible co-worker in witnessing.**
4. **You have demonstrated the kind of help that is available for those who mean business about serving Christ.**

With all this behind you, you are now ready to move on up the witnessing ladder. Wait until you see how all that prayer support pays off in the steps ahead. You may want to take "Time Out For Testimony" again.

Chapter Eleven

FEAR VS. POWER

You have reached the place where you can contact a total stranger, use a provoking phrase, and present a tract. You have also secured some prayer support. Beyond that, you have challenged others for the witness-life. That's real progress, isn't it? Wasn't it nice to find you didn't have to wait until the course was finished before you could ease others in to action? Since you are in motion for Christ, you just naturally stimulate others. It's a known law that motion begets motion.

> **CAUTION:** Satan is upset with you. Now that things are going well, you can expect him to try a trick or two. He may seek to infect you with a spirit of criticism. You know how that works. It follows the law of the harvest. If the devil can plant one little seed in your heart, it could grow to a full vine. It's amazing how an entire crop can be harvested from one tiny little seed. We do have to watch out for Satan.

The next time you are in fellowship with some IDLE brethren, check your heart to see what is going on. It would be very easy to observe those doing nothing for Jesus and think to yourself, **"Why don't those lazy Christians get off their seats and get going for the Lord?"** A slight amount of that is risky. All it takes is a seed, and once it begins to grow, it is hard to stop.

> **RECALL:** It wasn't too long ago that you were a sitter yourself. Be thankful that you have been delivered from the "sit and listen" tradition and your life is counting for Christ. Replace any criticism with compassion. Set your heart to help God's people. It is only as we love them that we can help them. Besides, they don't need our judgments, they already have a Judge.

● This time you are going to OPENLY IDENTIFY yourself with the Lord. And it will be the result of words from your lips. So far you have worn pins and let tracts speak of the Lord. You have not identified yourself as a Christian except as you were associated with the tracts. This time you will. But don't start trembling. Wait until you see how I want you to do this. I assure you it won't overstress you. This action stands squarely in the path of your advance. There's no way around it, so don't try to avoid it.

ACTION

Introduce into your daily speech pattern a reference to the Lord. There are any number commonly used and the public is somewhat accustomed to them. Phrases such as "Lord willing, I'll see you tomorrow," or "The Lord has sure been good to you," are typical of what I mean. You may already have an expression that is fairly natural for you. It doesn't matter what phrase you use, as long as it contains a reference to "The Lord."

"LORD WILLING, I'LL SEE YOU TOMORROW."

NOTE: This really isn't as threatening as it seems. I am not asking you to use the name, "Jesus." That would be overwhelming. All I want you to do is employ the term, "The Lord." You will find the public is used to the words, even

151

if you are not used to saying them. In fact, you may be a little startled to find how reluctant you are to refer to "The Lord" in a public encounter. I'm hoping you'll face it honestly if this proves to be the case. It's the purpose of this course to help you overcome it. Again, I want you to believe you are ready for this action.

The reason we deliberately incorporate a reference to "the Lord," is to focus attention on YOU as a Christian. Your phrase is not intended to draw comment from others so that you can witness to them. At this point, I am interested only in your personal feelings when people become aware that you are a Christian. We're going to turn the spotlight on any DISCOMFORT you feel when people look at you, knowing you belong to Christ. Will you get some reaction? It's likely. But you are going to learn how to **handle it**.

SARCASM

We've already noted that Christ is not popular. Religion is popular, of course, but Jesus, Himself, is not. While we will refrain from using His name in this lesson, we will be referring to His TITLE. People will notice. The Holy Spirit sees to that. So expect some comment as well as curious looks. They should come:

"What's this Lord stuff? Are you one of those religious fanatics?"

"I guess some people aren't happy without religion."

"You can thank the Lord if you want to, but He's never done anything for me."

"Don't give me any of that Lord talk, I get enough at home."

"I doubt if the Lord has anything to do with it at all."

It could be any kind of a remark containing a tinge of sarcasm. When it comes, you could have uncomfortable feelings. I'm not saying you'll get a reaction everytime you mention the Lord. For the most part you won't. But there's always the threat of it, and that's what makes our lesson valuable. Instead of a comment, you could get a sarcastic look. That carries the same message, doesn't it?

• Now the word (or look) has come. A flush rises to your face. You feel warm around your collar. You've gotten a reaction to "The Lord." Now what? Take a look at your feelings. It's a mixture of embarrassment and shame, right? I thought so. That's natural. No one likes to be deprecated. So, for a moment anyway, you feel terrible inside.

Scorn hurts. That's the price of open identification with the Lord. Maybe you already feel a little cringy inside as you read these lines? Perhaps you're glad you're not in a public place suffering rejection because of the Savior? That's natural, too. We're going to learn what to do about those feelings.

The other day I was in the checkout line at a local market. The man in front of me was bragging to me about his good health. He allowed that he had reached a bouyant 71 years through wise eating habits. I think he wanted a word of praise from me. I answered him with a witness line which included "The Lord:"

"I would be very happy should the Lord give me 71 years to serve Him!"

"Say, are you one of those religious guys who's always saying the Lord this and the Lord that?"

I felt the reproach of the Lord. I didn't like those feelings any better then, than I did when I first began to witness more than 20 years ago. The difference, however, is that now I knew what to do about them. **So will you.**

153

The instant the retort or sarcastic look comes, that is the moment to turn to the Holy Spirit. He has been present all along, of course, but now you enjoy Him in a different role. Now He is "The Comforter." As soon as you feel the slightest embarrassment, let that first flush signal your heart. Retreat to the sanctuary of your imagination and address the Holy Spirit, "Help me not to be ashamed of my Savior." He will, like this:

1. The moment you silently voice that request, He grants an awareness of His presence within you.

2. His "still small voice" asks, "Would you rather have this man's approval or Mine?"

3. The answer is not so automatic. It puts you in the place of decision and you feel it. You must decide on the answer.

4. From the valley of decison you can say, "I want to please you, dear Lord, and not this man." In that same instant you will have an awareness that God is watching you. He will send a flood of comfort to your heart.

5. Under the adoring gaze of your Heavenly Father, you sense this encouragement, "If you are willing to bear My reproach, I will join you in the experience. The two of us can handle it fine." (1 Thess. 5:24).

6. The anointing of God is like armor. From within the fortress of His presence, you may now look directly into the eyes of your tormentor. Don't be afraid. Your stare is anointed. Watch the strange expression that comes to his face. The Spirit of God is working in that man. You can see it. That's power.

7. If there is embarrassment now, you are not the one who is suffering. Your tormentor is feeling the witness of God. Don't be surprised if he apologizes.

...all this takes no more than a split second.

• Here we leave the matter. In a later lesson we'll deal with the man's apology and how to turn it into a powerful witnessing situation. For now, I am only concerned with your feelings. We are coming upon the matter of boldness. Real courage, you see, is not the absence of fear or hurt feelings, but what you are able to do about them in the presence of God.

SPIRITUAL MECHANICS

Working with the Holy Spirit like this, is a sweet science. But it is almost unknown today. Many have been so busy concentrating on the DOCTRINE of the Holy Spirit, they have forgotten He is a Person. In many places, He has been shoved aside by the same people who diligently seek to know more about His work.

A pastor came to my office last week and, in the course of the conversation, said to me, "How do you stand on the doctrine of the Holy Spirit?" I knew what he meant, of course, but it was a perfect opportunity to demonstrate the difference between the doctrine and the Person.

"I don't believe it!"

"**You don't!**" You should have seen the look on his face. What beautiful shock! Then I eased him. "I believe in the Person of the Holy Spirit." He was a gracious Christian and responded warmly. He believed as I did. Yet, it was good for both of us to talk about the Spirit as a Person. It's easy to learn doctrine. But what a difference between being able to list the functions of the Holy Spirit and to see Him do them before your eyes!

• That's what we're doing. Witnessing takes us beyond doctrine and into the science of working with the Holy Spirit—**at close range.**

1. Recall how I said the power of God works like power steering on your car? You turn the steering wheel and the power unit moves the front wheels. The power operates SIMULTANEOUSLY as you move the wheel. This is the way it works when we go into action for Jesus. When you elect to please God, rather than the man in front of you, you turn the wheel. God moves as you move. That's what takes care of your embarrassment. This is a demonstrable fact.

2. Boldness does not come in advance. No one can pray for boldness and then say, "Now I am bolder." It doesn't work that way. The Christian must first be in the place of actual witness and faced with the choice of pleasing men or God. Then—the boldness comes as he OBEYS. There is no shortcut. Boldness follows obedience.

3. Does that sound as if you shouldn't pray for boldness? We should indeed pray for boldness. All the time. But hear me carefully. There is no such thing as an infilling of the stuff because we pray. It just won't happen. But you ask, "Doesn't God honor such a request?" Indeed. But not, however, until we make a move toward a prospect. Boldness is not given in advance.

Listen to some of the requests at your next prayer-meeting. You'll hear people say, "Lord give us boldness that we may witness for Thee." Ah, but what do they really mean? They are saying, "Give us boldness AND THEN we will witness for You." Sorry, God won't answer that request. He says, "My command is for you to GO. . .you do that first. . .and I'll GO **with you.**" That is the unalterable formula for power. Boldness is the **reward** of obedience. If you tarry for boldness, it will never come. If you are waiting on God to fill you with boldness BEFORE you obey, you'll be tarrying for the rest of your life. On the other hand, if you GO first, you'll find yourself anointed with power such as you never dreamed.

God often waits until the last minute to answer requests. But you know that. Daniel was already in the lion pit before God delivered him. Abraham was ready to plunge the knife into Isaac's heart before God intervened. It was so with the people of Israel at the Red Sea. And again with the disciples in the boat as the "ship was covered with waves." God makes a practice of delaying His answers so as not to interfere with the discipline of obedience.

Let's look at this in another context. Consider the man with a temper problem. He cannot prayerfully commit his temper to the Lord and then assume the matter is settled—that God will somehow fill him with the spirit of self-control. He faces the matter every time he is tempted to "blow his top." It is only when he is confronted with an actual situation that he can DECIDE what he is going to do about it. If he wants to please God, he can expect help. So it is with boldness. The Christian must be in the place of witness before he can honestly decide to please God rather than men. As soon as he makes the right decision, the Holy Spirit moves.

NO ARGUMENT?

This truth is established by experience. We're not arguing doctrine here. We're beyond that. We're dealing with the PERSON of the Holy Spirit and He is ready to prove Himself to anyone who will try Him. Put yourself in the place of witness. You can test what I am saying here. You will be proving Him, when you do, not me. So when you feel that first tinge of embarrassment, decide right then to please God rather than those watching, and see if boldness doesn't sweep your heart. Unless you are in the place of witness, it just won't happen—no matter how much one prays.

157

Since this truth comes by experience, it cannot be gained by reading this book. I can state the fact that God will reward your obedience with boldness and power—if you look to Him for it. But you will have to put yourself in the place of embarrassment and fear in order to prove His faithfulness. He won't let you down. If He could fail you here, He could fail you in other matters, too. But He won't. And what does that tell us? It is the Holy Spirit Who finally makes witnessing easy!

> **NOTE:** Scorn and ridicule are such powerful feelings we will do almost anything to avoid them. The only power that can overcome them is the power of God. We need an anointing which is greater than our fear, a grace which is greater than all our dread. Therefore, this lesson on handling rejection in the power of the Holy Spirit is vital to your witnessing future. Please don't short yourself by taking it lightly.

ASSIGNMENT

Let the anointing of the Holy Spirit scatter your feelings of embarrassment ONE TIME and you're on the road to witnessing with your whole life. Taste the overwhelming triumph of standing in God's power, and it will no longer matter what men might say. Your fear is not cancelled, it is simply **overshadowed** by the greater experience of God's anointing.

But I want you to do this more than once. Plan on using the phrase, "The Lord," in your ordinary conversations at least **seven times**. Hopefully you can do this in a week. Here are three instances which should be fairly comfortable for you:

a. You can initiate a comment on the weather by saying, **"The Lord has given us another nice day, right?"** Weather is one thing we have in common with those around us.

b. Clerks sometimes ask, "How are you today?" An easy

reply would be. . ."**Just fine, thank the Lord.**" You'll find that to be a socially acceptable statement.

c. Cashiers often hand back your change saying, "Thank you, come again." You can reply with, "**I'll do that, Lord willing.**"

THEN—if you get a sarcastic reply or a scornful look, speak to the Holy Spirit at once. Decide to please Him rather than shrink from the scorner. Suddenly your eyes will be anointed. I want you to look full into the gaze of your scorner without flinching. Take God's power by faith. Now study your man. He is suffering. He cringes under your gaze, for the Lord has touched your eyes! Your look will pierce his heart. The Spirit will squeeze his soul.

Your prospect may apologize. He's been hurt. You will not know what is happening inside that man, but the convicting power of your divinely anointed stare is awful! Try it at least once, if you have any reason to suspect you are the object of ridicule. That's all I will require. No one will be able to stop you after you have had this amazing experience.

> **NOTE: I hope you will take as much time as you need for this rung. Please don't be in a hurry to move on. If you will work on this until you are satisfied the thrill of the Spirit's power is greater than your fear, you won't be sorry. You really need it. Rejection is everywhere. It is the stock and trade of aggressive Christianity. This world resents Jesus and anyone openly identified with Him. So replacing your fears with power is a vital part of the skill.**

We've spent a long time talking about two words, "The Lord." But those two words can bring fear and embarrassment. And fear and embarrassment have all but silenced the army of the Lord. So get your feet solidly planted on rung no. 6 of the witnessing ladder and your life will take on a new glow. You now know a lot more about moving in the power of God. Soon you will be touching the hearts of men and women with an anointing that is great—simply great!

Chapter Twelve

A BILLBOARD FOR CHRIST

Wowee! Wasn't that last lesson something! What a thrill to see our fears vaporize in the presence of God! It sure makes a person appreciate the Lord's willingness to fortify us against scorn. We live in Satan's world. Rejection is a real part of the life to which we have been called. That is why it is precious to discover **by experience** just what the Holy Spirit will do for us.

Yet—doesn't it make sense? I mean, when people like ourselves are the victims of feelings so powerful they can silence our lips against speaking out for Jesus, we need outside help. Just as a brain surgeon cannot operate on his own brain, neither can we overrule our own fears. God has to help us. How wonderful then, that "He rememberth that we are as dust" Psa. 103:14.

● In this lesson we're going to widen our identification with the Lord. Just as a new doctor arriving in the community hangs out his shingle to announce his presence, so will we. We're going into business too—for Christ. That is, we will advertise ourselves as belonging to Him. Obviously, we can expect an increase in threat.

> **NOTE: Do you experience mild shock as you think of open identification with Christ in a world that hates Him? You could. This is contrary, you see, to the way most Christians behave. The majority of believers gathers in church buildings once or twice a week to worship Him behind closed doors. After they step outside those four walls into the world where they have been ordered to witness, they become as silent as tombs. All week long they rub elbows with scores of lost souls, yet not a word for Jesus escapes their lips. Their efforts are spent the other way, keeping their identification with Him a secret. Obviously then, it is not the easiest thing for a Christian to oppose the mainstream of Christianity and move in the opposite direction. But it**

has to be done if we're going to please God rather than men. Besides, it hasn't been too bad so far, has it?

Have you noticed some of the posters carried about by young people involved in the religious rebellion? They read, "Jesus is for real!" or "Christ died for you, why not live for Him!" and sayings like that. These youngsters are fired with the spirit of revolt. For many religion is a gimmick, a current fad. But that's not true of all of them. Some are truly "turned on" for the Lord. And their occupation with Christ makes them almost fearless as they advertise their stand. True, they often work in groups and that does make it a lot easier.

But you're going to be doing your advertising by yourself. That is, you and the Holy Spirit will work together. Intimacy with the Spirit of God is going to do for you what being with the crowd does for "turned on" young people. That's why our last lesson was so vital. You had to know the experience of anointed EYES and the ARMORING of the Spirit in order to taste your real power in Jesus. Once you find you can face scorn in His might, you are ready to widen your identification with Christ. We couldn't consider such a thing until you sampled the Spirit's presence as a fortress against ridicule and rejection.

A BILLBOARD FOR CHRIST

You have reached the place where you should begin thinking of yourself as a billboard for Christ. I use that word because you are familiar with those great big signs that are too big to miss. Even so, the advertisers are careful to make their ads attractive as well as provocative. That's the way I want you to stand out for Christ in your own private world. You should be too big to miss. Yet, your advertising should be done in a way that not only gains attention, but commands respect and admiration. We can be billboards for Christ and be sophisticated about it.

161

Now here are seven good areas for posting yourself as a billboard:

- Your car
- Your home
- Your job or office
- Your clothing
- Your shopping routine
- Your public prayer
- Your speech

That's not all of your life, but it represents the biggest part, I'm sure. If we can get you posted as a billboard for Christ in those areas, we will have made good progress toward full time Christian service.

> **NOTE: It is common for Christians to think of "full time" service as having to do with the ministry or holding a job with a Christian organization. That is a satanic deception. Every Christian is called to serve Christ "full time," no matter what kind of a job he has. If he is a minister, he must still stand out as a billboard within his private world. Those employed by Christian organizations must also advertise for Christ in all these areas or they are NOT "full time" for Christ. A missionary is not full time for Christ by virtue of his job. He must also advertise throughout his private world before he is full time. No one is "full time" for Christ until he goes to work on making his whole life count for the Lord (Col. 3:23).**

Now let's consider the above areas one at a time:

❶ **Your car.** Think of all the people who see your car. Why not use it for Christ? He gave it to you. Everything you have belongs to Him (Rom. 12:1, 1 Cor. 6:19). It is a shame to drive about, letting multitudes see the car God gave you, without a hint of acknowledgment. Shouldn't there be some credit for Christ? At the very least, shouldn't there be a tasteful bumper strip on the back? They're so popular now, there's hardly any sting in displaying them.

Besides, Christian bookstores all over the land are beginning to stock them. If you really believe God has supplied you with a car, then He is due some public credit for it. It should be part of your billboard.

My daughter, who belongs to the "turned on" generation, unashamedly displays two of them on the rear of her car. One reads, "Jesus—bridge over troubled waters." The other says, "Join God's forever family." Others in my congregation use one which says, "Honk—if you love Jesus." God's people really honk at each other. The one I have on my car at the moment is a little more subdued. It reads, "Christ is YOUR answer."

So much for the outside of your car. What about the inside? Personal Christianity has developed a very effective dash warning sign. Here, I'll let you read it for yourself:

WARNING!

RIDE IN THIS CAR
AT YOUR OWN RISK

DRIVER COULD VANISH
ANY INSTANT!

To mount it, simply peel off the protective backing and press it against your dash panel. It's printed on adhesive material. It'll stick. Once it's mounted, no one can miss it. And it's full of intrigue. No matter who your passenger is, his eyes will spot that sign the moment he gets in your car. As soon as you are rolling along, you can deal with him (saved or unsaved) using this technique:

"I see you noticed my sign. There's nothing to worry about. Here, read this. It will tell you what to do in case I vanish!"

With those words you bring forth a copy of the tract, "What To Do In Case I Vanish!" These tracts conveniently fit in the ash trays on most cars. That serves to keep one at hand. See item no's. 111 and 406 in the catalog. This tract is very effective for the unsaved. However, given to a Christian passenger, it will challenge him for the witness-life. When he sees how you are using your car for the glory of Jesus, he may be inspired to do the same. At least it will give you a chance to tell about the course you are studying.

② **Your home.** Has not the Lord also provided your home? Shouldn't it be used for His glory? Of course. Relax, I'm not going to ask you to drape a huge banner across the front which shouts, "Jesus saves!" That would be too drastic. But there are some things you can do to make your home a witness to every person who calls on you.

a. Mount a tract dispenser on the front porch. On the outside affix a little sign which reads, "Take one." You'll be happy with the way every salesman and peddler coming to your porch will take a tract, especially if you are not at home when he knocks. If you can allow a provocative portion of the title to show, it will be even more irresistable. My wife is constantly refilling ours. We use the title, "Religion Can Be Dangerous," with the word CAUTION showing as the provoker. See tract no. 408 in the catalog.

HINT: A rugged tract holder can be made from a discarded film holder from any Polaroid camera. They are thrown away otherwise. Remove the small sponge rubber flap which is merely stapled and behold you have a holder. Spray it with some gold paint or any color to match your decor and you have a nice tract rack that costs nothing.

b. Inside your front door, two more things can be done. Make yourself a small tract holder out of cardboard. Unloosen the switch plate which operates the light near the front door and slide the top of your tract holder under it. Then tighten the plate down and you have a mounted holder ready for action. When anyone talks with you at the door, you will always have tracts at hand to pass out. On the back of the front door, mount some framed motto which points to Christ. That way anyone leaving your home will see it.

c. It is easy to make a display of Bibles and Christian magazines on end tables and other places in plain view. However, the witness is more penetrating if your home includes an interest center that features the Lord, Himself, in some way. There are excellent "Head of Christ" paintings to be found in the Christian bookstores. Such a painting would definitely identify yours as a Christian home.

> HINT: Available from Personal Christianity is an outstanding color reproduction of an oil painting of the crucifixion. It would make a highly provocative interest center. It is reproduced below. The reproduction comes rolled in a mailing tube suitable for mounting in a standard 16" X 20" frame. It bears the title, "It Is Finished!" by Linda Lovett.

If you already have this reproduction, there is an accompanying tract available called, "The Riddle Of The Cross." See your PC catalog. When someone comments on your painting, an easy reply is, "The title of the painting is 'It Is Finished', but I like to ask my friends and guests if they know WHAT was finished?" Some visitor might even say, "Jesus died there for our sin." Regardless of the reply, it would be in order for you to say, "Actually it is a riddle. You'll find the answer inside this tract. Why not slip it into your purse (or pocket) and read it when you have a moment?" Of course, if you have the strength for a discussion about the cross, there's no need for the tract to be put away. This action will go smoothly if your tracts are located under or near the reproduction. (See p. 252 for instructions on framing the reproduction.)

NOTE: After you reach the top of the witnessing ladder, the same painting can be used to create a soul-winning interview. The dialogue would go like this: "The painting is called, 'It Is Finished,' but I like to ask my friends if they know what was finished? Jesus died for our sins on that cross 2000 years ago, but do you know how that finished work is transferred to men today?" Most people will not have the right answer, i.e., the same Person Who died there is alive today and brings His finished work into the lives of those who receive Him as Savior. But you don't say that. Instead you measure your prospect, "So that I don't tresspass your feelings in any way, I should first ask whether or not you have any interest in spiritual things?" That is the number one approach question of the plan in SOUL-WINNING MADE EASY. Once that question is asked, the interview is under way.

③ **Your job.** If your car stands all day in the parking lot with your Christian bumper strip displayed, that is your first on-the-job identification. If a small New Testament peeks above your shirt pocket, that is another. If those working alongside you hear you humming Christian tunes, that is still another. Your transistor radio tuned to a Christian broadcast at lunch time is further identification. When you are seen bowing your head in thanksgiving at mealtime, the identification is more complete.

167

NOTE: If your employer has a policy against overt witnessing on the job, you would have to limit yourself to the billboard display. However, if there is no stated policy, it might be well for you to work, for a time, as a secret agent. Then you could practice the skill of concealing tracts without being detected. Should you get caught and asked to stop, do so completely—as unto the Lord. He understands. After that, you can post yourself as a billboard, avoiding any actual witnessing situations. It is obvious, of course, that once you install yourself as a billboard you can no longer leave tracts in secret. Everyone would know who was responsible for them.

The displayed Bible

Are you an executive? Work at a desk? That desk can be an important outpost for Christ. People will notice a Bible on your desk. But what about employers who regard religion as a touchy subject? Satan could make any display of the Bible look like fanaticism. If you are prepared with a wise reply,

A CHRISTIAN OPEN FOR BUSINESS.

you can display your Bible openly without any threat to you or your job. Should your employer ask about it, here's what to say. . .

> "This job requires decisions. Some of them take real wisdom. There's more wisdom here (tapping on your Bible) than there is here (pointing to your head). It's wonderful to have the world's greatest source of wisdom at your finger tips."

The toughest boss would be pleased with that remark. It tells him you desire to bring the highest wisdom to your job. What employer doesn't want his people to bring wisdom to their administrative decisions? Besides, everything about your remark is socially acceptable. No one denies the Bible is the greatest book in the world. But that must not be the end of your witness. When the Holy Spirit indicates a prospect is at hand, it is simple to exploit the situation provoked by your Bible:

> "Now that you've mentioned it (that shifts the responsibility for the discussion to the inquirer), some of the wisest people in the world depend on this book. In fact, this book can make someone like you or myself one of the wisest men in the world. (Then, reaching for a copy of tract no. 414, 'Wisest Man In The World,' you add. . .) And here's how it's done."

This witness can be performed with perfect freedom. Having the right answer on your lips turns a risky situation into one of relaxation. Wisdom can make a witness possible where zeal alone would create trouble. The Holy Spirit is ready to impart this kind of wisdom to those willing to advertise Christ throughout their private world.

4 **Your clothes.** Your witnessing pins (question mark pin, elevator button, etc.) are not Christian identification. They are provokers. They invite inquiries, but they do not mark you as belonging to the Lord. There are all sorts of pins and accessories that can advertise you as a Christian. A gold cross is a common example. A tie clasp is another. Lately a new trend in Christian symbols has appeared. Beads with crosses attached, large gold wire fishes, as well as huge buttons with bold declarations are now sold in the bookstores.

Since you are getting bolder, you might wish to identify more openly with Christ. From time to time I wear a pin that reads, "Jesus Christ changed my life!" I don't suggest you wear that. I mention it to show the trend. Different ones in my congregation wear badges reading, "Smile—Jesus loves you!" or "I found peace in Jesus Christ" or "Jesus—the only way!" For your personality it could be that a distinctive ring or cross is all you could wear comfortably. I do want you comfortable in your advertising for Christ. If you're not, you won't stay with it.

❺ **Your shopping routine.** We have already covered this, but now see it as part of the total picture. The moment you press a tract into someone's hands, you are identified with its message. Inasmuch as you are a little bolder, why not let the top of your tract titles show above the rim of your pocket. Consider the first few words of the "Religious Fanatics" tract. If people saw a piece of paper which read. . ."How to get rid of. . .," wouldn't they be curious to know the rest of it? Their minds would be asking, "How to get rid of what?" Someone might be curious enough to ask. It's happened to me a number of times. It's another way to advertise.

❻ **Your public praying.** When you bow your head to give thanks before beginning a meal in public, people never mistake the identification. Everyone is impressed by the humble dignity of unashamed worship. People never sneer at someone giving thanks to God. Addressing God, you see, is not the same thing as talking with a prospect. People may react when you talk to them ABOUT the Lord. But they are more awed than offended when they see you speaking directly TO the Lord.

Dr. Paul Gupta, president of the Hindustan Bible Institute in India and a former schoolmate of mine, and I were having lunch together at Clifton's cafeteria. It was time for the blessing. Paul removed his turban. Then he leaned back and unashamedly gave thanks to God with a loud voice. And I mean loud. I was peeking through the fingers of my hands as they shaded my eyes. There had to be a reaction. All around us people stopped eating. A hush settled over the large dining room. Waiters halted with their trays in mid-air. I don't know whether I was embarrassed or just startled. Maybe both. But I sure saw the advertising power of public prayer.

A line of people formed at our table. One after another told what it meant to see a man unashamed of his Savior. A number of the waiters were Christians. They were so encouraged by Paul's example, they pledged themselves to start witnessing more on the job. Our table was so busy with people addressing their thanks to Paul, it was difficult to finish the meal. But it was worth it to hear so much open talk about Jesus.

Now I don't tell that incident with any hint that you should turn yourself into a prayer spectacle. I merely want you to consider the advertising power behind letting people see you thank God without shame. The more dignity you bring to it the better. A short prayer is sufficient. The Spirit will use it as He pleases. But be sure to do it. You may feel a little awkward at first, but that merely gives you further opportunity to experiment with the Holy Spirit's presence.

NOTE: Should you raise your head from prayer to find someone has been watching you, don't shift your eyes away as though you are suddenly embarrassed. Instead look directly at him. As you do, speak to the Holy Spirit. Let His presence come over you like a flood. Then see what the combined testimony of your action plus HIS witness does within that spectator. The watcher will not only look away, his mind will be forced to consider spiritual things. This is extremely powerful when done in the Holy Spirit. Once you taste the power of this, no one will ever persuade you to stop.

7 **Your speech.** So far, the words "The Lord," have been the only open identification in your speech pattern. We began by using those two words because: (1) they are socially acceptable, (2) doing so left you more free to experiment with the Holy Spirit. Now we're going to widen your speech pattern to increase your billboard display.

One man speaking to another is the most impressive tool in the Spirit's arsenal. There is no greater influence than the force of one personality upon another. The Holy Spirit can use printed tools, even circumstances, but He would rather use YOU. He enjoys taking the simplest words and weaving them into a message just right for the listener's heart—with power. That's FUN for Him. I'm not talking about sharp, calculated witnessing lines. We haven't reached that point yet. I mean rather ordinary phrases which are not too threatening. It is amazing what God can say to a person when we give Him a few simple words to work with.

NOTE: All preachers have this experience. Often I have had people speak to me after a service and say how much they enjoyed the message. Then they'd go on and mention something in particular which I know I DIDN'T SAY. What happened was, the Holy Spirit took what I did say and shaped His own message. It meant one thing as it came from my mouth, but it registered as something very different in the listener's heart. So often does this happen I am convinced the Spirit of God rephrases our words far more than we suspect. He has the power to turn them into something just right for the listener—when we trust Him for it.

● This time we're going to extend your speech pattern by adding three new categories. They will be used as part of your

172

everyday conversation. Each category is a little more threatening. Your advertising becomes more penetrating as you do them. Note how they begin away from yourself and move closer and closer to an outright statement of identification:

a. **Invitations to church.**

We'll say you are in a shop or store (any kind of a business establishment). It would be natural to comment to the clerk...

"You're not open on Sundays, are you?"

"No, we're closed Sundays."

"That's nice. It gives you all a chance to get to church. By the way, I trust you have a church. If you don't, I'd like to invite you to mine. Here, the address is written on the back of this tract. See? Right there."

Of course, you don't have to use those precise words. I mean only to give you an idea of the way you can advertise your church and yourself with a reference to Sunday. If the store happens to stay open on Sundays, it's easy to shift your words around:

"I see you stay open on Sunday. I guess that means you don't get out to church much. Maybe sometime when you are off or close early, you'd like to visit mine. Here, the address is stamped on the bottom there."

NOTE: Your prospect may not have the slightest interest in visiting your church, but people appreciate being asked. Besides, you have placed a tract in his hands and any appreciation he feels is automatically transferred to it. It should get a good reading because of the influence of your personality as you showed an interest in the prospect. Also, you have advertised yourself. In the mind of many, church-going is the same as Christianity. For lots of people, to say you are going to church is the same thing as announcing you are a Christian.

173

To prepare for this action, check with your church to see if they have a rubber stamp you could use for stamping your tracts. If so, take a number of them to the church office and affix the name and address in the blank space following the message. There's room at the end of "Religion Can Be Dangerous," for example, which is a good tract for this purpose.

b. References to prayer.

Often we find ourselves around people (friend, neighbor, clerk) who are complaining of their situation or have made an error of some sort. They might even be protesting their circumstances or just grumbling. It would be a simple matter to say, "Say, I'm going to have to pray for you." You are serious, of course, but your big smile and the inflection of your voice suggests you are joking.

> NOTE: Your half-serious expression takes away most of the threat for you, and your smile and voice inflection prevent any offense to your prospect. Regardless of the humorous setting, these are serious words coming from your lips. Saying them in a light-hearted situation prepares you for more serious action later on. As casual as the scene may seem, your reference to prayer will penetrate the prospect. He will not be offended, yet he will reflect on what you said. After you have gone, the Holy Spirit will change the quality of your words from a joke to a jab—if you ask Him to.

If you want your witness to go deeper, then put your name and phone number on the bottom of a few tracts and have them ready. Set yourself to press the reference to prayer a little further. Like this:

> "Maybe I shouldn't kid about praying for you. You might have a big problem and I wouldn't know it. Listen, if you find yourself in a situation where you do need prayer, here's my name and phone number, right there. Give me a call. I'd be glad to pray for you."

174

You've produced your tract and your finger points to your name and phone number at the end of the message. Your prospect will not only accept it from your hand, he will treat it with respect. Likely, he'll give you his thanks, promising to keep it. You can be sure he'll read it, and when he does, it will be with emotion attached to the truths.

c. Mentioning God's Word.

You've finished your shopping. The clerk has given you your change. You are about to leave the store. Your hand is reaching into your tract supply. But first you say these words:

"I'm a Christian and I like to leave a bit of God's Word wherever I go."

There—saying that is the most threatening action on this rung of the ladder. Yet, it isn't as difficult as it sounds—and for a very good reason. The mention of GOD in your phrase AFTER you mention yourself, moves the spotlight from you. God is so much more important than you, the very mention of Him shifts the focus from you. He overshadows you. Ordinarily you might think it increases the threat to mention God, but it doesn't. It actually reduces it.

This time I want you to use the phrase exactly as I have stated it. It has been tested over the years. You'll find it easy to use as soon as you have tried it once.

NOTE: The authority of this action is tremendous. You are going to thrill to the way the Holy Spirit moves to give you favor in your prospect's eyes. At once you'll see he has respect for you and your tract. He'll treat that piece of paper with reverence, for he unconsciously assumes God is the OWNER. It will be as though your prospect is saying "Wow! Thanks!" You can be sure he'll read it. And along with it a sense of dealing directly with God. There's an aura of holiness about this approach with a tract. You'll have the sense of being God's prophet as you do this in His power.

WAYS TO BE A BILLBOARD

1 YOUR
CAR

2 YOUR
HOME

3 YOUR
JOB

4 YOUR
CLOTHES

5 YOUR
SHOPPING
ROUTINE

6 YOUR
PUBLIC
PRAYING

7 YOUR
SPEECH

Please don't be afraid to try this action. It might sound hard as you read about it here on this page. But it really isn't. In fact you are going to be surprised just how easy it is. The Holy Spirit gives plenty of help with this one, when you trust Him for it. The hardest part will be getting yourself to try it. After that, it gets easier and easier. And you will be delighted with the new strength that comes to your spirit. Think what it will mean to your soul to be able to say without fear, "I am a Christian, and I like to leave a bit of God's Word wherever I go."

ASSIGNMENT

When you reach the last rung of the witnessing ladder, you will be organizing your whole life as a witness for Christ. There you will be thinking about the use of your TIME. Right now, however, we are only concerned with PLACES. We have discussed seven places, or maybe I should say, seven FACES of your billboard. I will be very happy if you can think of yourself as a billboard for Christ standing squarely in the middle of your private world. If you operate successfully, people will mark you as a Christian no matter where you are.

● The purpose of this lesson is to condition you to see that NO PART of your weekly routine is untouched by the Great Commission. Your whole life should be geared to witnessing for Jesus. While I am not going to give you any specific assignments concerning your car, house, job, clothes, etc., I do want you to DO SOMETHING in each category.

> NOTE: If you don't drive or even have a car, then you can't advertise in that area. If you are a housewife who doesn't work away from home, then you can't witness on the job. In that case you probably spend most of your time at home. Therefore, you should concentrate on making your home an impressive witness for the Lord. If you spend much time on the phone or chatting with neighbors or participating in activities, those would be areas for posting your billboard. Ask the Holy Spirit to show you how to fit every area of your life into your big display for Christ.

But when it comes to YOUR SPEECH, I want you to do each of the actions three times. That is an assignment. Plan on giving three invitations to church, making three references to prayer, and refer to yourself as a Christian three times. This is a must. If you goof off, you will not gain the strengths you need for the next rung up the ladder. So, even if you slack off on the other areas, do not fail to do the speech exercises. They are vital. So much for the assignment.

DO I HEAR A QUESTION?

"How do I respond to people who ask about my advertising?"

Has that thought crossed your mind? Are you wondering what you will do when everyone sees your billboard and starts asking questions? I can tell you right now, very few people will say anything to you. Why? Is it because they don't see your advertising? No. People are reluctant to discuss spiritual things. It brings thoughts of God to their minds and that makes them uneasy. Thinking about God brings conviction to unsaved people. Discussing Him is even more painful.

But you are a billboard. There you stand advertising the Lord. Yes, you are a sophisticated disturbance. And some will ask you about it. However, you will be more comfortable as a billboard if you are prepared to answer the occasional soul who might ask about your display for Christ.

If someone asks about your car, pin, or praying, etc. . . . here's how to reply:

"I'm glad you asked me that. Let me answer you with this. . ." (Hand him the tract, "Since You Asked").

"What's this?" (That could be his reaction.)

"You asked about the slogan on my car (badge, Bible, etc.) **and I think this will give you a better answer than I can."**

• Being ready with that kind of an answer eliminates having to think up one on the spot.

At this point on the ladder, you are not required to drive home any pointed statements about the Lord. Neither are you trying to extract any comments from your prospects. That comes on the next rung. In this lesson I want you free to watch your feelings and handle the reaction that comes from your wider identification with Christ. If you start thinking about using all of these various areas of your life for the Lord, we will have accomplished our purpose.

What is more thrilling than total forgiveness and absolute peace with God? Nothing. "There is no peace for the wicked," says God. But now you have complete peace with Him and it's glorious. So think about this. We get excited at ball games. We shout and scream for our favorite team. We don't even consider how funny our antics are. Do we not make ridiculous gestures and say ridiculous things to amuse a baby? Sure. Then, if Jesus is the most astonishing fact of our lives, what's wrong with letting it show?

Nothing! And you know it. It's just that until now you have been afraid to show your delight in Him. But with this study, the Holy Spirit is making it possible. Soon you will find yourself talking about Jesus with as much joy and flair as you can about a vacation trip or a new car. It's getting involved with the Spirit of God that makes it easy to publicize our relationship with Christ.

You're going to like the idea of open identification with Jesus. Why? You are going to be so proud of His faithfulness and power in your life, you'll want everyone to know of your joy. And do you think you will ever be sorry?

"He that confesses Me before men, him will I confess before the holy angels."*

---

*Luke 12:8

179

Chapter Thirteen

THE PREPARED WITNESS

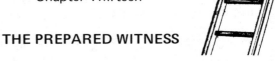

We reach a turning point in the ladder-method as soon as you post yourself as a "billboard for Christ." On rung number 8 you will no longer be waiting for people to come to you asking about your advertising—you will go to them. By now you have discovered how few people respond to your displays, even though many notice them. Therefore, it is important that you become more aggressive in getting the gospel into their hands.

There is hardly a situation a Christian meets in the course of his daily routine that can't be turned into a witness—**if he knows how.** That's the purpose of this lesson. You are going to learn how to TURN common, everyday encounters into witnessing opportunities. It is a skill, but once you get the hang of it, you'll like it. Besides, it's fun in the Holy Spirit! You don't really see God's power, as you should, until you become a little aggressive for Christ. Aggressive witnessing is not the art some think it is. For most of us, it is more properly described as a skill.

WITNESSING ISN'T AN ART?

"I don't think Christians should bother with planned witnessing. I sure don't need any kind of a plan. I just make up whatever I want to say to people right there on the spot!"

You should have seen the brother who told me that. What a super-salesman he was! So bold was he, and so loaded with social gifts, he could have sold me anything he had in his pockets. Did I believe his claim? You bet. He could witness without any help from anyone. Who could hold him back? He dominated every person he met.

Are most of us like that? Far from it. We are timid souls who won't open our mouths unless we know what to say and how to say it. Most of us are NOT witnessing artists. Of course, there are those with a talent for approaching strangers and speaking of Christ. For them witnessing is definitely an art. But I assure you, such people are few and far between. So rare are they, we shouldn't speak to the average Christian of the ART of witnessing. We do better to speak of witnessing as a **science.**

Our colleges and universities distinguish between the arts and the sciences. You know the difference, don't you? Art departments seek to develop those talents **already** within a person. But the science departments, on the other hand, equip people with methods and mechanics. The ungifted person could never become an artist no matter how long he studied. There is no way to generate gifts where none exists in the beginning. Most of us have to approach witnessing as mechanics, not as talented Christians.

Have you ever met a witnessing artist? He's something else, isn't he? He needs no help from me. It's easy for him to create a new approach every time he meets a stranger. His personality gifts make it so simple for him, he can't understand why the rest of us don't do the same. How many people do you know like that? One, two perhaps? Could you copy them? No. Prepared witnessing is more like it for us. As far as we're concerned, the Holy Spirit is the real Artist and we have our hands full learning to work with Him. We have to be methodic about it, or we won't do it at all. Without careful preparation, we remain silent. But is that so strange? Haven't we already learned that God honors **preparation?**

PREPARED WITNESSING

Below you will find a series of dialogues and situations which anyone might encounter in a routine trip from his home. Watch how they can be turned into witnessing opportunities. As you read, picture yourself as the witness performing the action. Let your imagination become the classroom. See yourself as saying these things to a prospect.

If you are by yourself, read the lines aloud. Note how the threat increases as you advance through the list. Don't hurry. Give your imagination a chance to work. Don't try to memorize any words, just picture the scenes. Visualize them as taking place in familiar spots within your private world, say a beauty parlor or on the job some place.

Some of the dialogues may seem awkward to you. Others will feel comfortable. What is easy for one person could be difficult for another. So, of the 20 dialogues you will be reading, perhaps five will seem natural for you. Out of those five, one or two will fit your personality nicely. Later, I will be asking you to select at least five of them and use them in the assignment. That much will give you a starting point. Then, when you get the hang of it, you can develop your own dialogues.

> **NOTE:** Think about this. If you can get the key word of a tract title into any conversation with an unsaved person, you can easily turn the interview into a witnessing situation. Be watching for that as you go through the scenes. Don't be disturbed that a tract is still presenting the main message for you. Believe me they do a terrific job, often a better one than we can do. What we're concerned with at this point is using your LIPS to turn a typical conversation into a witnessing opportunity. That is the point of this lesson.

● Here then are the dialogues much as I use them myself. Notice how they exploit common matters, such as the weather, time, and how one feels.

1. How often do people say to us:

"Nice day, isn't it?"
"I'll say. I wonder if we'll have days like this in heaven?"
"I wouldn't know."

"Perhaps it doesn't matter anyway. The important thing is getting there, wouldn't you say?"

"Yeah, maybe so." (Or similar response.)

"Here, you ought to read this. It doesn't explain the weather in heaven, but it does tell HOW to get there."

[Offer any good salvation tract that presents the mechanics of salvation.]

2. When someone asks:

"Could you tell me what time it is?"

"According to my watch or according to the Bible?"

"Your watch, of course."

"By my watch it's 5 o'clock, but according to the Bible it's time for everyone to wake up. Here, this will tell you why it's risky to wait until the alarm goes off!"

[Present tract no. 415, "Some Are Sleeping."]

3. Again, when people ask:

"Would you happen to have the correct time?"

"Our time or God's time?"

"Our time."

"It's 2:35 p.m. our time, but according to God's time, it's never too late until death shuts the gate. If you want to make it, you'd better get on the elevator."

"What elevator?"

"This one (as you offer tract), the elevator of life!."

[Use tract no. 421, "The Elevator Of Life."]

4. People are always asking:

"What's new?"

"What kind of news do you like—good or bad?"

"Good, I guess."

"If you're serious about hearing good news, I'll tell you what it is. Good news is an old English word for the gospel. Did you know that?"

"No, I didn't."

"Okay, here then, is the good news: Christ died for our sins and we can have total forgiveness by receiving Him as our personal Savior.

This will tell you how. This is the most important headline you'll ever read!"
[Tract no. 401, "The Riddle Of The Cross" would be suitable. Or any salvation tract that speaks of forgiveness.]

5. Here's the common greeting:

"Hi, how are you today?"
"Oh, I'm much better now, thank you."
"Have you been sick?"
"Oh no, but down at our church we sing 'Every day with Jesus is better than the day before.' So, I'm better today than I was yesterday."
(Any kind of a flustered response may come.)
"It really is great to feel better every day. I'm sure you would like it yourself. Here—read this—it will tell you how!"
[Offer any tract that tells how to become associated with Jesus. The "I Feel Great" tract would be fine, though any good salvation tract would do.]

6. Here's another common greeting:

"How are you doing?"
"Okay, for a fanatic!"
"Awh, you're no fanatic. . .are you?"
"Perhaps not, but isn't that what they call people who think the Lord is terrific and want to share the Christian life with others?"
"Oh, I don't know about that."
"In any case you don't have to worry. Here's how you can get rid of me."
[A big smile as you present tract no. 428, "How To Get Rid Of Religious Fanatics!"]

7. Suppose the weather is gloomy and someone says:

"Sure is a miserable day, isn't it?"
"Sure is, why don't you ask the weatherman to change it?"
"Awh, he can't do anything about it."
"In that case you ought to read this. It will put you in touch with the One Who makes all our weather in the first place!"
[Offer any tract that presents Christ.]

8. In a crowded place someone bumps you accidentally:

"Oops, I'm sorry." They mean it, too.
"That's okay, accidents will happen. Or maybe it wasn't an accident?"
"What do you mean?"
"It's possible we were supposed to meet like this so I could give you this!" (Offer tract.)
"What's this?"
"I don't mean to embarrass you, but it could be God's way of having you bump into Christ. If that happens, it will be no accident. It will occur just as it is written there!"
[Use no. 407, "Would You Be Embarrassed?"]

9. When showing off your wallet full of family pictures, make the last one in the list a head of Christ.

"Here's my family. . .(go thru the list). . .but I'm not the head of our house."
"Oh? Who is, your wife?" (If a woman, this won't be asked.)
"He is. . .Christ! Ever since we turned our home over to Him, our family life has been wonderful! Here, read this. Maybe you'd like to know what Christ can do for your family."
[Use any salvation tract that speaks of Christ and the family. . . whether in heaven or on earth.]

10. When your change back includes pennies:

"Well I see I get back some pennies. They don't buy much any more do they?"
"I'm afraid not."
"I know of one bargain you can still get for a penny—people's thoughts. Haven't you heard the expression 'A penny for your thoughts?'"
"Yeah."
"Well, I'm a thought buyer and I'd give a penny for your thoughts on this!"
[Give back one of the pennies to the cashier and along with it, tract no. 416. . ."A Penny For Your Thoughts."]

11. When approaching a check stand or gas station attendant and you are wearing a no. 482 Monkey pin, ask the clerk:

"Are you open for business?"
"Yes, we're open."
"Good, so am I as you'll notice from the pin I'm wearing."
"Oh, what kind of business are you in?"
"This is my business."
[Wear a big smile as you offer the tract no. 417. . ."Monkey Business."]

12. Occasionally a clerk returns too much change:

"You gave me back too much money."
"Oh thanks. It's nice to meet an honest man."
"I should thank you. You see, I'm a Christian and you gave me an opportunity to do something pleasing to the Lord. So here's my special thanks—in writing."
[Present tract no. 411. . ."Thank You." The words, "my special thanks," explain your action.]

13. Again, when a clerk returns too much change:

"You gave me back too much money."
"It's nice to meet an honest man for a change."
"There was a time in my life when I would have kept it. But since I became a Christian, the Lord has been turning me into an honest man. So, you really should give the credit to Christ. I hope you know Him well enough. If you don't, this might get you acquainted."
[Present any salvation tract that explains HOW to receive Christ.]

14. While the friendly gas station attendant is filling your tank, ask:

"You don't allow people to smoke while getting gas, do you?"
"No. See the sign there? It's against the law."
"I don't blame you. It could be plenty dangerous. But you ought to read this. Here's something more dangerous than a gasoline fire."
[Use tract no. 408. . ."Religion Can Be Dangerous." It will harness the risk of fire with the risk of false religion.]

15. When a store clerk approaches and asks:

"May I help you?"
"Yes, if you'll allow me to help you in return."
"What do you mean?" or "How would you do that?"

"If you're kind enough to help me find what I need, I ought to return the favor and help you find what you need. Aren't you curious to know what it is?"

"I think I have an idea, but go ahead anyway."

"Good. I'm glad you're curious. Here it is. And it might be just the thing you need."

[Present tract no. 426. . ."Curious?"]

16. Someone has just exclaimed:

"For heaven's sake!"

"Hey, I'm glad to see you're interested in heaven. What have you done about getting there?"

"I don't know, not much I guess."

"I know I'm going there, and something like this helped me to make sure of it. Here, read this. Maybe it will do the same for you."

[Offer a good salvation tract that tells HOW to get to heaven.]

17. Occasionally someone asks for a light (cigarette).

"You wouldn't happen to have a match, would you?"

"I don't use them since the explosion."

"What explosion is that?"

"The one that took place in my life when I became a Christian. Now I have another kind of fire inside me and I don't need cigarettes any more. You look like a wise man to me. Why don't you try this instead of a match. Perhaps it will start a fire in you and you won't want cigarettes any more either."

[Offer tract no. 414. . ."The Wisest Man" or any good tract that speaks of an experience with Christ.]

18. When someone asks God to damn (swear) something:

"Do you think He will?"

"Will what?"

"Do you think God will damn that, like you say?"

"Awh, go on." (He's embarrassed).

"No, I'm curious. God's name is precious to many people. I was wondering why you used it. Do you know Him?"

"What do you mean?"

"Like I said, I'm curious. Would you want someone to swear by your name or even your mother's."

"If I offended you, I'm sorry."

"Maybe I'm the one who should apologize. I see I have embarrassed you. But one day God is going to ask you about it and that could be really embarrassing. Maybe you'd better read this. It could save you from being embarrassed in that day!"
[Present tract no. 407...."Would You Be Embarrassed."]

19. When it's a wrong number on the telephone:

"Is Rick there?"
"No, there's no one here by that name."
"I'm sorry, I must have the wrong number."
"Just a moment. Weren't you surprised to hear a strange voice."
"Well, sort of."
"I don't say this to startle you, but you're going to hear another strange voice. Someone else is going to call you up."
"Oh, who?"
"God is going to call you up to stand before Him one day. And it won't be nearly so frightening if you get acquainted with Him ahead of time. Would you like to know what the Bible says about getting ready for that call?"
"Yes, I think so."
"If you'll give me your name and address, I'll send you something from the Bible that will tell you exactly how to get ready for God's call."
[Send the booklet, "Your Biggest Decision," no. 107 in the PC catalog.]

20. When you wish to start a spiritual conversation with an employee in a store, ask:

"How do you like working here?"
"Oh, it's a job, I guess."
"How would you like doing this kind of work forever?"
"Not me. They can have it."
"I don't blame you, it probably wouldn't be the best job in heaven. But then I guess we'd have to agree that getting there is more important than the job we have there, wouldn't you say?"
"I suppose so."
"Then you'd better read this. It won't mention your future job, but it does tell how to get to heaven."
[Present any salvation tract that tells HOW to get to heaven.]

SEE THE ADVANCE IN SKILL?

The idea of calculated phrases is not new to you. You have used them in past lessons. And so far, the most threatening phrase for you was, "I'm a Christian and I like to leave a bit of God's Word wherever I go." That was a stock phrase used to explain the passing of a tract. But this time we're interested in phrases which, when inserted in an ordinary conversation, instantly turn it into a witnessing opportunity. That's a very different use of the calculated phrase.

Here again is the principle: interject the key word of a tract title into the conversation, and you are in a position to create a witnessing interview.

Consider the KEY word of a few of our PC tracts:

DANGER . . . . . . "Religion Can Be Dangerous!"
FANATIC . . . . . "How To Get Rid Of Religious Fanatics"
WISE . . . . "The Wisest Man In The World"
EMBARRASSED . . . "Would You Be Embarrassed?"
QUESTION . . . . . "Answer The Big Question"
GREAT . . . . . . "I Feel Great!"
RIDDLE . . . . . . "The Riddle Of The Cross"

● Get any of those key words inserted into a conversation and then a calculated phrase can be used to get the corresponding tract into the hands of a prospect. It sounds simple, doesn't it? It is, once you acquire the skill.

It really doesn't matter which tract you use. Perhaps you already have a favorite of your own. All you need do is lift the KEY WORD from the title and develop two phrases. One for introducing it into the conversation, another (based on that key word) for getting it into the hands of your prospect. That's the skill we're learning in this lesson. It is an advance over anything you have done so far.

NOTE: If your favorite tracts have such words as "forever, time, eternity, heaven, life, death, etc.," it is easy to develop a fascinating phrase for shifting the conversation to that very topic. After that, you need another phrase, based on that topic, which makes it natural for you to offer the tract. Let me repeat an earlier caution: avoid using any tract which does not tell people HOW to be saved. It is a waste of time and money to use tracts that do not spell out the mechanics of salvation. You will leave your prospect frustrated, if you do.

THE ELEMENT OF DANGER CAN BE USED FOR THE LORD

DID YOU PICTURE YOURSELF IN ACTION?

As you went through the list of 20 dialogues, did each scene come to mind? Did you see yourself in the actions? Did you notice how the conversations were manipulated? The use of KEY WORDS made it possible to shift the conversation from secular matters to spiritual. Do you see how it would be possible to use a few of these 20 dialogues in some so your own daily contacts? I hope you do. But let me say this, nothing about those dialogues is rigid. I vary them all the time when I use them myself. It's the principle behind them that is important, not the reciting of a fixed set of words.

Once you get the idea behind the development of these phrases, you can create dozens of them for yourself. I've furnished these simply to give you the hang of it. Those you prepare for yourself will be better suited to your personality than those I've developed for my use. Therefore, it is important that you learn the principles for creating the phrases. At the same time, though, there is nothing wrong in your using those I've set forth here. If you can't develop any of your own, by all means use these.

Besides the main principle of the KEY WORD, here are three more:

a. Using questions. A prospect's pride compels him to answer questions put to him. None of us likes the idea of appearing to be ignorant or unlearned.

b. Harnessing emotions. Fear, curiosity, embarrassment are emotions which can be triggered within a prospect and then used to reinforce the truth of a tract. And you will discover other emotions that are useful as well. What is vital, is knowing that truths clothed with strong emotions do a startling job in a prospect's spirit.

c. Developing questions. You can create questions for which the reply doesn't matter. That is, you are prepared to handle the prospect's answer no matter what he says. In such cases, it is the FACT that he responds, that is important. For then you can ease him to the next step. For example, "Do you get embarrassed easily?" can be answered with a yes or no. But it doesn't matter since you can lead into your tract from either one.

● Now then—what do you think about putting this skill to work in your life? Can you see yourself developing phrases that would cover almost any situation you might encounter in the course of your weekly routine? The moment I say that, I'm sure an annoying question comes to mind:

"If I learn to use such a skill, will I be expected to witness to every person I meet?"

Ouch! That could bring a stab to your heart. So let me answer quickly. NO. Such a thought could be used of Satan to keep you in the house all day. But as soon as I say that, another question comes to your mind. "How, then, do I know WHEN to witness to a person?"

The Holy Spirit is the answer to that question. He understands us so well. Loving us, as He does, and knowing our weakness and fear better than we know ourselves, He does not overstress us. His leadership is gentle. He knows how much we can take and still ENJOY the witnessing business. You see, it is to the Lord's advantage for us to find witnessing an adventure, not a terror. He wants us to thrill to the Great Commission, not be terrorized by it. Only then will we purpose to stay with it for the rest of our lives. That's just good business on His part.

NOTE: The Lord does not mean for His commission to threaten us. He simply asks us to prepare ourselves and be ready for those moments when our strength and desire to obey Him match the opportunities He sends our way. There is nothing frightening about that. He advances us gently and gradually, wanting us to experience the thrill of working with the Holy Spirit each step of the way. So relax. Trust Him to design opportunities that are just right for you. He really does want us to enjoy working with Him at close range. He is wise in this. He knows we'd soon give up if witnessing didn't bring us the promised satisfaction for our souls.

ASSIGNMENT

Are you ready for action? Good. How will you begin to apply what you have learned? That's easy, by beginning with the dialogues I have furnished. That is, out of the 20 which I have furnished, I would like for you to select FIVE that appeal to you and use each ONE TIME. I am assigning five actions for this lesson.

Now let me qualify that. If you have caught on to the idea of developing your own phrases and can come up with some that seem more natural for you, then change the assignment to read: two of yours and three of mine. I'm sure you can pick out three of the 20 that will fit you comfortably. We're not that different from each other.

> HINT: As soon as you have selected your dialogues or worked up some of your own, type them off on 3 X 5 cards for easy carrying on your person. That way you can use any spare moment to review them and keep them on the tip of your tongue. If you select the "wrong number" dialogue, tape it to your telephone. Also, I am secretly hoping you'll try the "Fanatics" dialogue. It works beautifully for me. Not only does it generate humor, which cancels threat, but it is fun to watch the way people act when you brand yourself a fanatic. It takes the wind out of their sails.

Now plan to be a little aggressive. That's the new feature on this rung of the ladder. Go after some people rather than waiting for them to come to you about your advertising. Be on the lookout for prospects when you go to the gas station, market, beauty parlor, or job. Someone is sure to say, "How are you today?" Be ready to pick it up and move in on him. Now that you are able to turn any normal conversation into a witnessing situation, nearly everyone around you becomes a prospect. But again, I am not asking you to overstress yourself. Besides, FIVE times is hardly an overburden.

As you present your tract, commit both your prospect and the tract to the Spirit of God for His blessing. Keep yourself in touch with the Lord even as you talk with your man. The Holy Spirit will bear witness to the fact that you seek only his spiritual prosperity. You should have no trouble at all. In fact, I expect you to find this action FUN, the very first time you try it.

● Does that sound so hard? I haven't asked you to give any kind of a personal testimony. Neither have I required you to ask anything of your prospect. All you are to do is make DELIBERATE moves toward 5 people within your private world and create a situation for getting the gospel into their hands. For this, you will use short, pre-planned phrases. Don't be afraid to try. The Holy Spirit will embolden you the moment you open your mouth to speak. Watch and see if this isn't so.

> **HINT:** Do you think it would be easier for you to begin these actions in the company of your prayer-partner? It is fine with me if you'd like to do the first one together. Everything is easier when Christians do them together. There is the added strength that comes through knowing your partner is talking to the Lord even as you speak to your prospect. I do want you to do at least four of the actions entirely on your own.

Secure a little notebook that you can carry on your person. Now that you are shifting over to more aggressive action for Christ, the Holy Spirit will be giving you unusual ideas for turning normal conversations into spiritual interviews. You will find some remarkable words

coming from your lips as you speak to a prospect. That will be due to God's anointing, His blessing on your obedience. Plan to capture those ideas on paper.

After an interview is over, take a few seconds to record anything that appears unusually wise you have said. When we go into action for the Lord, God's anointing AUTOMATICALLY follows. Sweet inspiration comes when we obey. So don't be surprised if you find yourself coming up with fresh ways of turning conversations to Christ. But write them down. Those precious things are born in heaven and they usually come our way but one time. If you capture them on paper, they are yours to use again and again, but if you don't, and they are forgotten, you lose them forever.

YOU WERE WARNED

Didn't I warn you not to read past page 58 unless you meant business for Christ? Did I not say, "Read no further unless you are determined to go on and become a witness for Jesus?" Indeed I did. And now you see why.

What Christian can read these scenes and not see himself in various situations? All of them are opportunities that come to us continually. And now you KNOW HOW to use them for Christ. Such knowledge brings responsibility. No, you shouldn't have kept on reading if you didn't mean to press on for Christ.

You now have in your possession some startling knowledge. Surely you realize the possibilities of what you have just learned. Here is sufficient know-how to turn your life into a flaming witness for the Lord. No longer can timidity, fear, and ignorance be your excuses for disobedience. From now on you are faced with one question, **"Do I love Jesus enough to stir myself for Him?"** That's what it boils down to, for you have the know-how you need. If you love Him, you'll put it to work. It's a jolt when it comes like that, right?

Besides, the Holy Spirit is going to prod your conscience. Every time you encounter a prime witnessing opportunity that is just right for you, the Great Commission is going to well within you. Why? You now possess what you need to carry it out. Wouldn't it be awful to face God in that day with no fruit, because you didn't care enough to use the skills He gave you? It would, indeed.

Remember what happened to the lazy steward in the parable of the pounds? (Lu. 19:22-24). You wouldn't want that to happen to you, would you? Of course not. Well, let's face it. The only reason you would not move out for Christ after reading these pages is because you simply don't care about doing His will. That sounds harsh, I know. I'd much rather say I am persuaded of better things of you. I believe you do care. You wouldn't be reading this book if you didn't. So I am confident that you are going to do MORE than I ask of you here, much more. And it is because of this confidence that I sense we are ready to move on to the highest witness. That's next.

Chapter Fourteen

THE HIGHEST WITNESS

We now come to the peak in witnessing. I suppose that frightens you. Relax. Most things sound harder than they really are. You've learned that by now. This too will be easy, once you see what it is and try it. But you're wondering, just what is the highest witness? I'll tell you. It occurs when you have told another person:

1. **I'm a Christian,**
2. **I have received Christ as my Savior,**
3. **I know my sins are forgiven,**
4. **I'm on my way to heaven,**
5. **God will do the same for you if you'll give Him a chance.**

Weave those five elements into a conversation with an unsaved person and you will have gone as far as one can go in witnessing. The next step is to ask the person to do something about it. However, when you do that, you leave the business of witnessing and move to the work of the soul-winner.

Do you recall what we said earlier about the person on the witness stand? He merely tells what he knows. He is not the prosecuting attorney. He gives his witness and that's all. The witness never seeks to manipulate a prospect or press him to **do anything** about Christ. Getting people to act on the Lord's invitation is the work of the soul-winner.

Consider that word, "manipulate." That's a proper word for soul-winning. The soul-winner operates like a salesman, maneuvering people to a decision. He knows how to make people face the Lord and decide about Him, one way or the other. His techniques are very different from those of the witness. He is a specialist in closing the deal for Christ. But the witness has no thought of doing that. He merely passes on what Christ means to him. It's the task of the witness to

197

plant the truth of Jesus in a prospect's heart and let the Holy Spirit take it from there.

Therefore: we reach the highest point in witnessing when we explain what Christ will do for those who give Him a chance.

YOU'RE READY FOR THE HIGHEST WITNESS

Until you acquired the knack of converting routine conversations into witnessing situations, you had to rely on short, pat phrases for passing tracts. But now you have the means of engaging anyone in a conversation and shifting the focus to spiritual things. This time the spotlight is going to be on YOU. You are the provoker. You are the highest witness.

Will you still use tracts? Indeed. Tracts are vital even on this rung of the ladder. Today's witness cannot afford to be without them. They do a job the witness cannot do, no matter how sharp he becomes in speaking about the Lord. No one can put a witness in his pocket and take him home, but a tract will accompany a person anywhere and say its message again and again. Tracts won't dilute the force of your highest witness, they actually reinforce it. So now the fun is going to increase as you speak words about yourself in the power of the Holy Spirit.

NOTE: In the last lesson you learned the principle behind using phrases for turning conversations into witnessing opportunities. You should continue working on those phrases, refining the ones I gave you as well as creating new ones of your own. It is acquiring skill in the use of calculated phrases that makes you a poised and sophisticated witness. Your strength lies in your ability to EASE into spiritual interviews no matter what kind of a conversation is under way. Now that you have learned the power of carefully worded phrases, work hard to put a keen edge on them. Perfect them. The more skilled you become, the bolder you will be in the Spirit. These phrases and tracts,

used in combination, comprise the sharpest witness method today.

• As you practice with your phrases, discovering by experience how wonderful they are for **easing** into a spiritual conversation, your joy will increase greatly. The easier it becomes, the more natural will become your witnessing. You'll find yourself able to make the most penetrating type of witness, yet never offending your prospect. That is real sophistication. It's true that you may have to start with the phrases I have supplied for you, but the Holy Spirit will show you more which are even better for you.

ENTHUSIASM

Again I must observe that enthusiasm is the magic ingredient. Now that we have come to the highest witness, enthusiasm is more important than ever. Since the witness tells what he knows is true of himself, he uses the personal pronoun frequently. A man should be very enthusiastic about his relationship with Christ. If he is, the prospect is more apt to be infected with his message. Enthusiasm is highly contagious.

Before you approach your prospect, say to yourself, **"This is going to be an enthusiastic presentation."** Say it silently several times. Then feel the grin appear on your face. What a way to start! You're in the greatest business in the world. Shouldn't it show? Sure. Christians have every right to be enthusiastic when they talk about Jesus. They know by experience what it means to be forgiven of every sin and be heaven bound. So think enthusiasm. Walk enthusiasm. Talk enthusiasm. Then your witnessing will sparkle.

NOTE: Enthusiasm can be developed. You can turn yourself into an enthusiastic Christian simply by acting like one. The moment you start to act like an enthusiastic person, your own self-image changes and you become enthusiastic. "As a man thinketh in his heart, so is he." It's as simple as that. Once you see how mightily the Spirit can use your

199

enthusiasm in witnessing, you'll refuse to appear any other way. Besides it's fun—and any nervousness you have disappears. That's right. Enthusiasm has the power to overrule nervousness. Wait and see.

Yesterday, I arose from a swell night's sleep. I just knew it was going to be a great day. As I chatted with the Lord, I sensed He meant for it to be an outstanding day. All this bubbled inside me before I left the house. My first stop took me by a small store. It was early. I must have been the first customer of the day.

"How are you today?" The clerk was friendly, but still sleepy.

"Great, simply great!" (I had been talking to myself about enthusiasm.)

"How come you're so peppy this morning? Get up on the right side of the bed or something?"

"No, this is just a great day and I'm caught up in it. Since you're the first person I've met, you'll probably add to it!"

"I doubt that. Not much ever happens around here."

"Say, you're not missing out on the excitement of life, are you?"

"Maybe I am."

"That's a shame. I was like that once. . .back when I lived in the rat race of 3 meals a day, on the job, back to bed, day after day. You know, the same old routine, and for what? Boy, did I ever get rid of that life. I traded it in for the most exciting life there is. You know what it is, don't you?"

"What?"

"The Christian life. Everyday can be exciting when you get to know the One Who made you. That's big stuff. Besides

He's got a thrilling plan for each of our lives. He's got one for you, too. Did you know that?" (See how asking that question keeps the conversation from drifting off target?)

"Yeah?"

"Sure, even the grave can be exciting when you're a Christian. Ever think about dying?"

"Yeh, but I don't see how anyone could think it was exciting?"

"You can when you take Christ as your Savior and know that your sins are forgiven. When you know that everything is okay between you and God, the grave is the last day of school. I'm not kidding. Right now I'm involved in the greatest adventure of this world and the next. Death is nothing but graduation day for me."

"I can tell you are excited, all right."

"You would be too if you gave Christ a chance to show you His plan for your life. It's a great thing to be a Christian. Here, read this. It will tell you more about it."

"There must be something to it if it can make a man feel like you do."

As I left the shop, I looked back to see my man. There he was with his elbow propped on the counter, his chin resting in his hand. He was going over that tract for all he was worth. Fortunately there was no business. It was a good witness. My enthusiasm stood out in sharp contrast to his boredom. He FELT the difference between us.

NOTE: See now what the highest witness is—YOU! When you reek with enthusiasm, there is a sharp difference between you and the one receiving your testimony. That difference is strategic. People can't miss it. They feel it. You want them to feel it. Without it, you can't really give the highest witness. For people CATCH what you are as well as HEAR what you say. Enthusiasm gives your witness striking force. It pays off big.

Well, my next stop was the post office. I drove around in the back, wanting to drop off a number of parcels at the loading dock. A postal clerk was piling some mail sacks at one end of the platform. I'd seen him a number of times before. He came over to help me unload the parcels.

"Hi," he greeted me pleasantly. "I've been meaning to ask you about that pin you wear. Some sort of a bird, isn't it?"

"Yes, it's a dove, the Bible symbol for God's Spirit. It was nice of you to notice. What did you think it was?" (That keeps the conversation flowing.)

"I thought maybe it might be an eagle and you belonged to some sort of a club or lodge."

"No, I wear it for another reason. When someone like you asks about it, it gives me a chance to tell about the fantastic thing that happened in my life."

"What's that?" (He takes the bait.)

"Since you asked, I'll tell you. For years I was haunted by the idea that there had to be more to life than 3 meals a day, on the job and back to bed. I felt like a squirrel in a cage going through my routine for no apparent reason. Then one day someone showed me something in the Bible that explained what was missing in my life. You know what I did about it?"

"What?"

"I believed what the Bible had to say about Christ being the Savior, so I opened my heart to Him and asked Him to come into my life. The moment He did, I knew every sin in my life was forgiven and I was on my way to heaven. He will give you the same experience, if you ask Him."

"You know, I thought you would probably say something like that. That's really why I asked about your pin. I've been thinking I ought to do something about getting right with God."

I wasn't expecting that. But God had placed this tender heart directly in my path. What happened next is not really a part of WITNESSING MADE EASY. It belongs in the area of soul-winning. I will tell you that I shifted over to the Encounter Method, as set forth in SOUL-WINNING MADE EASY. The man invited Christ into his heart then and there. But you can see how the witnessing conversation set the stage for the soul-winning situation, can't you? This time it was my PC pin that initiated the interview, yet I did move in with the highest witness. From there I went into the soul-winning plan.

● That conversation contained all the elements of the highest witness. I told what I had done about Christ and what He had done for me; and of His willingness to do the same for my prospect. It could have ended right there. The witness was concluded. It was only because I knew how to escort a soul through the experience of receiving Christ, that God used me for the next step.

A FEW WORDS — A CHANGED LIFE!"

NOTE: Did you notice the use of questions in the above dialogue? They control the conversation. The first one, "What did you think it was?" forced my prospect to speak further about the pin. The second, "You know what I did about it?" forced him to inquire. That is the power of technique. It compels your prospect to say what you want him to, and it allows you to complete your witness.

I have shown these two cases simply to let you see how the elements of the HIGHEST WITNESS can be woven into a conversation. The trick, though, is to be able to take ANY introductory remark and turn it into a situation whereby you can give your witness. See now why I want you to work on those calculated phrases? They make it possible to create a witnessing scene and give your witness.

Consider some usual greetings:

1. What's new with you?
2. How's everything with you?
3. How are you today?
4. How's it going?
5. How are you doing?

Many greetings run like that. If you wanted to be even more direct, you could reply with:

"If I dropped dead right now, this would still be one of the greatest days in my life!" (Can you see yourself saying that with enthusiasm? Then add the hook.) "Do you know why?"

"Why?"

"I'm a Christian, I have Christ as my Savior. My sins are forgiven. If I dropped dead right here in front of you, I know I'll be with the Lord. Could a man ask for anything more wonderful than that?" (Again the power of the question).

"No, I guess not." (The prospect could be a little flustered).

204

"I don't know how you feel about the Lord, but I can tell you this: He'll do the same for you if you give Him a chance!"

● See—all I did was get around to saying "greatest day of my life" and bait the prospect to ask why. Then that opened the door for my highest witness. In fact, there is no way for a prospect to keep you from giving it. Even if someone called you a fanatic, you could come back with, "Yes I am, but do you know why?" Then give the five elements in your answer. Catch the idea? If you practice, so as to make yourself sharp with phrases, you can create an opening for the highest witness anytime you wish. However, you will find it wise to put a few good ones on cards and carry them with you. Practice with those that work best for you, and you'll be giving the highest witness all the time.

I walked into the office of my insurance agent. One of his clerks was at the counter. I saw him there as I was coming in the front door. I wondered if he might be a candidate for the highest witness. My spirit flashed upward to check in with the Holy Spirit. Then I gave myself about three shots of enthusiasm. That is, I said to the Lord, "This is going to be an enthusiastic witness, isn't it Lord!" Up went my grin. The clerk said to me automatically, "Can I help you?"

"You can help me with my insurance, but I doubt if you could help me to feel any better. I feel great today. Would you like to know why?"

"Sure."

"It's because I'm a Christian. I have Christ as my Savior. My sins are forgiven and I'm on my way to heaven. Shouldn't that make a man feel great?" (Again the hooking question).

"I suppose so."

"I don't know how interested you are in feeling great, but I can tell you that Christ is able to make you feel as great as I do, if you'll give Him a chance."

Since the man was alone at the counter, I didn't hesitate to come on with the highest witness. If others had been there, I might have used another approach. It could have embarrassed him. But privately, like this, it was strategic and powerful. It was easy for my enthusiasm spilled out of me. The awareness of the Spirit welled up within me. I sensed HE was enjoying it.

However, had I not chatted with the Holy Spirit about the situation and my enthusiasm, I probably would have cared for my insurance needs without saying a word to the man about Jesus. You see, C. S. Lovett has to maintain himself in the Holy Spirit or he will miss witnessing opportunities like everyone else. Though I've been at this for years, I am no bolder than my current intimacy with the Spirit. I have to keep myself aglow through constant fellowship with the Lord, or I will forget and forfeit many opportunities to exalt Christ. In this case, you'll note I was already speaking to Him as I walked in the door of the insurance office. But that wasn't the end of the scene:

"I hope I didn't embarrass you by speaking of the Lord."

"Oh no, it didn't bother me." (It wouldn't matter if he said yes.)

"I'm glad, for then I can give you this. It's great for people who don't get embarrassed easily."

ARE THE STEPS CLEAR TO YOU?

We've been through the highest witness several times now. I hope you have observed the four steps.

1. Coming out with your enthusiastic statement.
2. Baiting the prospect to ask why.

3. Answering with the highest witness.
4. Exploiting any generated feelings with a tract. The tract also tells the prospect how to be saved.

But let's suppose the tract portion of that interview went like this:

"I hope I didn't embarrass you by speaking of the Lord?"

"Well, I'm not used to talking religion in public."

"I'm sorry. I didn't mean to embarrass you. Perhaps you will want to read this. It's perfect for people who get embarrassed about religion."

Now let's go through it again this time watching for the four steps. I'll let you be the witness this time, and I'll observe. Your imagination can again be the classroom. We'll pretend you have gone into the bank and have walked up to the teller's window. There's no one in line. The lady smiles at you. She asks, "May I help?"

"You sure can, if you don't mind waiting on a fanatic." (You wear a big smile, of course, as you say that) **"Or are you afraid to wait on a fanatic?"** (That's your hooking question).

"You're not really a fanatic, are you?"

"Isn't that what they call people who think the Lord is a terrific person and the Christian life too wonderful to keep to themselves?"

"I wouldn't know about that."

"I just assumed I was a fanatic, because I like telling people:

1. I'm a Christian,
2. I have Christ as my Savior,
3. All my sins are forgiven,

**4. I'm on my way to heaven.
In fact, I think it's fun to be a fanatic!"**

(Any reaction. It doesn't matter what she says.)

"If fanatics frighten you, read this. It will tell you how to get rid of them." You can be sure she'll accept your tract (no. 428).

5. "However, when you find out what God is ready to do for you, you may decide to become a fanatic too!"

There now, that wasn't so bad, was it? Of course, since you did this in your imagination, you were not able to feel yourself being filled with the Holy Spirit as the words were coming out of your mouth. I can tell you, the exhilaration is utterly fantastic. And it wipes out fear totally. Even without the awareness of the Spirit filling your being, didn't you enjoy doing that much for Christ in your imagination? Sure you did. Well, it is just that easy when you do it in public. You wait and see. The Holy Spirit has a treat in store for you.

OBSERVE: This won't apply to you yet, but it is interesting to observe how the presentation of a tract at the end of such a witness is a terrific technique for the trained soul-winner. Why? It serves to qualify a prospect. It tells the soul-winner what kind of an opportunity is before him. How? The prospect's reaction to the tract measures the situation. (1) If he throws it on the ground, he is hostile to the gospel. You couldn't reach him. (2) If he shoves it in his pocket, promising to read it later, he is probably not interested. (3) If he lingers to read it, you've got a possible on the string. (4) If he asks what church you attend, he is more than curious. (5) If he comments favorably about the tract, you've got an open door. So tracts are extremely useful even to the most skilled soul-winners.

● The scenes I have been describing in this chapter are presented about as they occur in my own witness-life. I have given that same witness, in varied form, hundreds of times. Sometimes it is abrupt and direct, other times it is carefully woven into the conversation. I can tell you from experience that it is just about as easy to come right out with it as it is to attempt a subtle weaving of words. Now you may not think you can do this as abruptly as I have shown it above. Again, you might not THINK you can. But I assure you, you can.

I guarantee this: try it once and you'll be surprised at the gush of POWER the Holy Spirit supplies when you open your mouth for Jesus. He moves as you move. You will be over-joyed with the way His presence wells up within you. You will be startled by your own boldness. I mean that. God is faithful. If your eyes are on HIM, instead of your fears and timidity, you will find yourself doing things which otherwise seem impossible. I cannot say it often enough—intimacy with the Spirit of God makes it possible to do amazing things for Jesus **with astonishing ease.**

THE RETURN VISIT

Let me anticipate your next question:

"What if I give the highest witness in a place where I often shop? Won't I feel funny facing the same prospect on my next visit? What will he think of me? Won't I feel embarrassed?"

Don't worry. If you went back to that same store a half-hour later, and met the same clerk, he wouldn't say a word to you about it. Know why? It would be too painful for him. For an unsaved man to think about you in connection with your witness would remind him that Jesus was ready to do in his life as He did in yours. That is not a comfortable idea for people resisting the Spirit's call. The only person who will mention your action is someone the Spirit has stirred with your words or tract. It will be a positive reaction.

So much for the way the prospect feels about it, now how about your own feelings?

It bothers you that the clerk MIGHT secretly consider you a crackpot. You can picture him saying to himself, "Oh oh, here comes that religious nut again." That's uncomfortable, isn't it? Well we can't have that, so here is a technique for taking all of the sting out of your return visit. I don't want you worrying about subsequent encounters with the people receiving your highest witness.

● You enter the store again. The same person greets you:

"Good afternoon, may I help you?"

"Sure, if you don't mind waiting on a fanatic. I wouldn't be surprised if that's what you thought I was." (He has to respond.)

"Naw, I wouldn't say that."

NOTE: This technique strips away judgmental feelings. When you call yourself a fanatic, those who would judge you are disarmed. It's a strange phenomenon, but when we defend ourselves, people are inclined to resist us. On the other hand, when we debase ourselves, people tend to rush to our rescue. You can watch this occur before your eyes when you use the "fanatic" technique. It works beautifully. A few self abasing words and your would-be tormentors shift over to your side. If you have not already given the prospect a "Fanatic" tract, you could do so now.

"Maybe I am a fanatic, maybe not. In any event you don't have to be afraid of me. In case I do turn out to be one (reaching for a tract) **read this. It will tell you how to get rid of me."**

See the humor in that? If you use that dialogue with a big smile on your face, it will cancel every bit of critical feeling your prospect may have stored against you.

HOW ABOUT THE THIRD TIME?

We've said you shopped in this store often. Now you are back again. For the third time the same clerk greets you, "How are you today?" Without batting an eye, say to him, "I'm just fine, for a fanatic!" Not only are you smiling, but there's a delightful twinkle in your eyes. The situation is very different now. The fanatic business is something of a private joke between you and your prospect. What was once a threatening situation, has been turned into a humorous relationship.

But that's not all that happens. Every time this person sees you, he is **unconsciously** reminded of the things you said. The words are no longer coming from your lips. They don't have to. He can see you. And seeing you is almost as powerful as hearing the words of your highest witness. The transfer is made. Your presence has now become the highest witness to him.

> **NOTE:** I use this technique continually as I go about my private world. Occasionally I meet someone whom I suspect feels I am unduly aggressive for Christ. Immediately I identify myself as a fanatic. Once that fact is out in the open, with SMILES, the contact no longer has any reason to harbor such feelings PRIVATELY. To date this technique has STRENGTHENED the relationships between me and those I see often, to whom I have given the highest witness. Not a person that I can recall, of all those who know me to be outspoken for Christ, really believes I am a fanatic. Not one.

PERFECTING THE APPROACH

By now you see that the difficult thing about the HIGHEST WITNESS is not learning or using the five elements, but creating a proper scene for saying them. The secret for setting the stage is having carefully worded phrases (on the tip of your tongue) which allow you to steer the conversation toward your witness. So, once again, we're back to those calculated phrases. See how vital they are for effective witnessing? Perfect two or three of them, and you'll be on your way as the highest witness.

As you look back over the ones I've used in this chapter, you'll find they had to do with:

1. Missing the excitement of life.
2. The fantastic thing that happened to me.
3. If I dropped dead right now.
4. You couldn't help me feel any better.
5. Afraid to wait on a fanatic.

Of course, they didn't appear just like that, for that would be meaningless. But woven as I used them, they do the job. Once you get the hang of it, you can develop those which match your personality. It might be hard for you to use the ones I use. Again, it might be easy. You'll have to determine that for yourself. My point, though, is this: armed with a couple of good approaches, you can create a scene for the highest witness any time you wish.

And what is the best way to master calculated phrases? Putting them on cards and carrying them on your person. Then, when you have a free moment, go over them until they are as much a part of you as your arm. That's what puts them on the tip of your tongue for instant use. **Once you have them down pat,** you'll find yourself working into the highest witness with ease. And you'll be ready for those times when the Spirit has prepared the circumstances for you.

Now if you DON'T perfect your approaches, you'll find opportunity after opportunity slipping by. Afterwards, you'll be kicking yourself, "Why didn't I take advantage of that situation and give my witness?" The answer: "You weren't sharp enough. You couldn't move fast enough, because you weren't ready with the phrase." Sometimes the opportunities require hair-trigger alertness on our part. If we're not prepared, they're gone before we know it.

NOTE: Please take me seriously when I ask you to put those phrases on 3 X 5 cards and learn them perfectly.

Practice and practice. Every skill takes practice. Witnessing for Jesus is no exception. If you wish to start with those I've given here, fine. Develop variations of them, if you like. You are not bound to use what I use, yet they might be a big help to you in getting started. That's why I have supplied them. Even though you start with lines and dialogues I have developed, you will graduate to your own in time. When you do, they will be the ones best suited to your personality.

• We're almost ready for the assignment, but there is something I want you to see first. Have you noticed how easily a person could go from the highest witness into a soul-winning interview? Not every one you meet is resisting the gospel. Sometimes your highest witness provokes very interesting responses:

1. I wish I had what you have.
2. I've felt for a long time I needed something in my life.
3. I used to go to church a lot, and I've been thinking I should get started again. . .etc.

People who respond like that are ripe for soul-winning. They are waiting to be plucked for the Lord. And there are quite a few of them around. I run into them all the time, so I know they are there. You're going to run into them too. A 10-year old could lead such people to Christ if he had the know-how. Therefore, I don't think it's too early for you to think about securing that skill for yourself.

After you've given your highest witness to a number of people, you're going to want to go further. I expect you to develop a longing to win at least one soul to Christ. The thing that haunts is that your witnessing comes right up the edge of soul-winning. You know the next step can't be that much harder. Especially when there are people hungry to be introduced to Jesus. So let's talk about that.

213

I'M GLAD I KNOW HOW

Once I stopped to pick up a young lad who was hitch-hiking. I opened the car door for him, "Come on in if you don't mind riding with a preacher." ("Fanatic" would have done just as well). As he scooted in to take a seat, I reached hurriedly to retrieve my Bible. "Oh oh, don't sit on my Bible." The lad paused so I could move it from the seat. Those few words paved the way for an opener. My next remark was easily in order:

"Ever have any contact with this Book or hear what it has to offer a person?"

"Yes, I have. In fact, I want to become a Christian, but I don't know how."

My car never got into high gear. We pulled over to the side of the road and in minutes he made a beautiful decision to receive Christ. What a thrill it was to hear him invite Jesus into his heart. Now let me ask, what would you have done? Huuuummmmmh? Was I ever glad I knew how to introduce a soul to the Lord.

● The point? You're all set for me to ask you to become a soul-winner, aren't you? I'm not going to do that, but I am going to suggest that you equip yourself with the KNOW-HOW for leading someone to Christ. Why? So that you will be ready for those moments when ANYONE could win souls—**if he knew how.** I mentioned this earlier, but now that we've come to the highest witness, we should talk about it more seriously. Some people are going to respond to your witness so enthusiastically, you know they only need the slightest shove to land in the kingdom. I would like to see you able to help them make that last step into Christ.

HINT: What would you do if a prospect responded to your highest witness with "Man, I'd become a Christian if I thought it would turn me on like you!" Taking such a man through the 4 steps would be child's play for a trained soul-winner. But you're not able to do that, yet. If you elect to acquire the skill of presenting Christ ALIVE, some time will pass before you master the technique. In the meantime, it is a good idea to carry a tool on your person that will do the job for you. "Your Biggest Decision" was written for this very purpose. It is the "Encounter-method" of soul-winning reduced to a booklet. It shows a man how to lead himself to Christ and test the decision afterwards. It's not the same as a face-to-face interview, but is a swell substitute until such time as you can deal with an eager prospect yourself.

Suppose there's a knock at your door in the wee hours. A voice cries out an urgent appeal. "Could you come? Mr. _____ is dying and he wants to talk to you!" After all, he's a neighbor and you're a Christian. You have to go. Sure enough, Mr. _____ is dying. His face lights up when he discovers you beside his bed. His feeble hand clutches yours:

"I'm afraid to die. But you're a Christian. Please help me. I want to go to heaven!"

What would be more awful than being in that situation unable to present your Savior to a dying man. There's no time to call your pastor. Besides, he asked for you. Dear friend, it would tear at your soul for the rest of your days if you watched that man expire without Christ, because you didn't know what to say to him. I know of Christians who have stood by helpless to answer a dying victim's cry for spiritual help. It haunts them to this day. We must not let that happen to you.

I hear what you're saying and you're right. Such a scene could be explained away theologically. On top of that, the chances of a death-bed appeal are remote. But not so remote is the possibility of someone responding to your highest witness with, "How can I get what you have?" or "I've been wanting to talk to someone about this very thing." What then? It's not very hard to talk to people who WANT spiritual help, yet won't expose such longings until they have received the highest witness. It is your witnessing at the face-to-face level that makes them admit their interest in spiritual help. And there you stand facing a golden opportunity.

So what am I saying? That every Christian should be a soul-winner? No. I'm saying that every Christian should possess the KNOW-HOW for introducing another person to Jesus, even if he **never uses the skill**. That's my point. I haven't told you to win souls in this book. I'm not saying it now. But I do feel strongly that you should acquire the KNOW-HOW. Please weigh my suggestion carefully.

I would like for you to order a copy of SOUL-WINNING MADE EASY. It offers a 4-step plan for presenting Christ ALIVE. The Holy Spirit developed the plan from thousands of personal encounters in my own life. I call it the ENCOUNTER METHOD, for the techniques clearly bring a prospect face to face with Jesus, and compel him to DO SOMETHING about Christ, one way or the other. Yet, it is simple. So simple, in fact, that anyone can learn it. Once he does, he is armed for any "emergency." This plan should be part of your spiritual first aid kit.

HINT: An easy way to master the plan is to secure no. 203 "Soul-Winning Demonstration Cassette" that dramatizes the dialogue. It presents an actual interview so that you can hear the transition lines as you go from verse to verse. Listen to the cassette over and over until the plan becomes fixed in your spirit. Along with listening to the cassette, you and your partner should practice leading each other to Christ until you can do it smoothly. Then, when the time comes and your know-how is needed, you'll have it. You'll be amazed at the way the Holy Spirit will bring it out of you in a "live" situation, when it lies burning in your Spirit. For details, see the back of the book.

ASSIGNMENT

Now it's your turn. Here's your assignment. I want you to give the highest witness to ONE person. That's right. Just one person. You're ready for it now, so don't be afraid to try. I know you feel a bit squeemish about starting, but the Holy Spirit is ready to back you to the limit. He cannot give you courage in advance. He never gives anything in advance of the need. So taking that first step boils down to trusting the Holy Spirit to fill you as you go into action. I guarantee you will thrill to His presence the moment you open your mouth. That is, if you chat with Him before speaking to your prospect.

"Are you sure you mean for me to give the highest witness just one time? Is that the whole assignment?"

Yes, I meant what I said. The assignment is done as soon as you give the highest witness to one person. You see, I know you are in for a thrill. You are going to be so overjoyed with the Spirit's anointing, you won't be satisfied without more. The power of God works like dope. Get a good taste of it and you're hooked. You'll want more, I know. Therefore, I am quite safe in asking you to do this only one time. Here's how I want you to go about it:

Let's say you have made a few selections in the market and now you are coming to the check stand. The cashier is alone and not busy. At once your mind goes to the Holy Spirit. Yes, He is indicating this is an opportunity for the highest witness. So you decide to act. That was all God needed. As your right foot hits the ground, you sense new boldness surfacing. When your left foot comes down, you hear. . ."Lo, I'm with you!" That's how fast God rushes in to bless obedience. This assignment takes more power than anything you've done before, but you have it. That's the Spirit's part. He never fails.

1. As you move closer to the checkstand, your pulse quickens. That's another signal. You flash a communication to Jesus, "Lord, work through me, and let's make this my most enthusiastic witness!" There's nothing He'd rather do.

2. Then your disarming smile appears. Make that grin big. It's a terrific tool for the Spirit. People do not fear those who smile. God's presence helps the smile. "I'm right here with you, son." You feel His breath upon your soul. There's no doubt. God is with you. You're not alone.

3. You speak first. . ."Hi. . ." Then comes your baiting phrase. I don't care which one you use, just make sure your enthusiasm shows. Then start through the dialogue.

4. It works! There is power! Hallelujah. You can actually see your words register with divine authority. It doesn't matter how your prospect reacts. He is being penetrated. The Spirit makes sure of that.

5. Wow! Feel the surge of power as you speak of God's forgiveness. The thrill of saying such things in Jesus' name sweeps your soul. Then it's over and there's that glorious "Well done." There's nothing like it in this world.

NOTE: Consider again the magic of enthusiasm. It works on you as well as your prospect. You are indeed excited about Christ. If you could have but heard yourself giving that highest witness. It was great. It wasn't an act. You really are delighted with the Lord. It showed, that's all. This excitement with and in Christ is going to change your life. Now will you believe me when I tell you you are going to be a fantastic witness?

● This rung of the witnessing ladder brings you to the peak of witnessing skill. I've given you the basics, the raw essentials for penetrating a man's soul with the news of Christ. There is no sharper or more penetrating type of witness than the one presented in this lesson. From here on it is a matter of perfecting what you have learned.

The more skilled you become, the more often you will be confronted with situations where you could lead your prospect to Christ, if you knew how. So I am hoping you will go beyond the highest witness and equip yourself with the "Encounter-Method" of presenting Christ ALIVE. In fact, I'm hoping that the Lord Himself will plant the desire in your heart. When He does, your soul will echo the words of a poem I love so well:

> "When I enter that beautiful City,
> —and the saints in glory draw near;
> I want someone to greet me and tell me,
> —it was you who invited me here!"

Next to the Lord's "Well done," those words on the lips of a precious soul in heaven, will be the most glorious sound we will ever hear. Wouldn't you like to hear them? I know you would. I'm confident that you are going to hear them. You wouldn't have come this far if you didn't mean to press all the way in Christ. If we're to go all out for Christ, we have to be business-like about serving Him. That's next.

Chapter Fifteen

GET BUSINESS-LIKE

We're here at last! You've reached the top of the ladder. You now have the sharpest witnessing know-how available today. But when you were starting out, did you think you'd make it all the way? I'm sure there were times when Satan had you thinking that systematic witnessing was not for you.

You had failures. You goofed lots of times, right? We all do. After each failure, Satan sends a wave of discouragement over our spirits. Discouragement is one of his most powerful weapons. Fortunately though, failures are a part of the learning process. They teach us lessons we cannot learn any other way. Much of what I have presented in this book, I learned after many failures. Some of it will be real to you only after you have failed.

FAILURES ARE IMPORTANT

If you fail to witness to the gas station attendant, for example, and later remember your failure, it can shock you to discover how far your mind had shifted from Jesus. When you fail to leave a tract after visiting the post office, you might ask yourself, "How can I be so immune to the Spirit's prodding?" If you can move among the people of your private world without seeing them as prospects for the gospel, it could make you ask, "How can I be so indifferent to Christ's command?"

See—failures can bring us up short. They can embarrass us inwardly. We should blush to find we care so little about Christ. We do, you know. We forget Him hours on end. Our witnessing failures prove to us how preoccupied we are with our puny errands, rather than our Master's business. Yet, if our failures can make us more determined than ever to live for Christ, they do us a great service. If we set ourselves to focus our minds on Christ, these failures can shame us into a closer walk with Him.

Who remembers Edison's 10,000 failures before he invented the electric light? Yet, without those failures, he would have never reached his goal. Each took him that much closer to his objective. And so with us. Each can make us more business-like about serving Him. So think of your failures as stepping stones to witnessing success. If you do, Satan will no longer bother you with feelings of discouragement. In time, Christ will be your career.

CHRIST—A CAREER?

Just a bit ago I had an exciting chat with a local business man who is also a Christian. When I saw the tracts on the counter in his store and the tract holder in his pocket, the conversation moved to the fun of using tracts for Christ. Here's what he said when I asked what using tracts had done for his life. . .

"Until I became business-like about leaving tracts where-ever I can, I had a routine Christian existence. But now I find that the Holy Spirit has become so real to me through this work, I wouldn't trade it for any other job in God's program!"

He glowed as he said that. I could tell he was a man who chatted with the Spirit constantly as he scattered the gospel throughout his private world. He'd rather talk about Christ than make a sale in his store. Christ was His career, his real business.

Allow me to lift an illustration from THE 100% CHRISTIAN.

My daughter, Linda, is infected with the thrill of witnessing in the Spirit's power. A few days ago I was her passenger as we headed for PC in her little red Ford Mustang. She was low on gas. I pointed to a station where we could stop. Her reply sent shivers of joy through me. . .

"No daddy, I have already witnessed to all the people in that station. I don't like to keep going back to the same place when there are other stations I haven't reached for the Lord."

I accompanied her while she drove a mile out of her way to fill up at a station where she had not yet witnessed to the attendants. Repeating that incident may sound like a father's proud boast, but Linda believes that Jesus owns her, lock, stock, and barrel. To her mind, there is no choice about obeying His orders. You bet I'm proud of her. Living for Christ is her career. Should you ask her about it, she'll quote a verse that is right on target. . .

"His purpose in dying for all, was that men while still in this life should CEASE TO LIVE FOR THEMSELVES and should live for Him Who for their sake died and was raised to life" (2 Cor. 5:15).

WE ARE ACCOUNTABLE

Each of us should feel the brand of Jesus' ownership on his soul. Christ owns us completely, having bought us at the price of His own blood. We are obliged to sacrifice our time and comfort in His interest. Is it really possible for a true Christian to feel no obligation to Someone Who does as much for him as Jesus? Now that the Holy Spirit has provided this simple LADDER-METHOD to obedience, there is even less excuse for ignoring His orders.

● For some reason there is silence across the church on the matter of our accountability at the Judgment Seat of Christ. You hear almost nothing about it, but of course that doesn't change the fact any. Perhaps the most sobering truth any Christian has to face is that one day he will stand before the Lord to give an account of the things he has done in the flesh.

"For we must all appear before the Judgment Seat of Christ, that each one may be recompensed for his works in the body, according to what he has done, whether it be GOOD or BAD!" (2 Cor. 5:10).

222

Surely it is going to go hard with those Christians who refuse to obey the Great Commission. I wouldn't want to be in their shoes as they stand before the Judge, trying to explain why they shunned His orders. That's enough to give a man the shakes. It actually terrorized the apostle Paul. He said so in the next verse:

"Knowing therefore the TERROR of the Lord, we persuade men" (2 Cor. 5:11).

The Judgment Seat of Christ is the most awesome fact of the Christian life. It struck terror to the heart of Paul. It made him business-like about reaching men for Christ. It would do the same for us, if we realized the consequences of disobeying the Great Commission. Again and again Jesus made it clear that we are His friends ONLY if we do as He commands (John 15:14). Those who disobey His orders forfeit the privilege of being close to Christ in heaven.

NOTE: A host of Christians is unconcerned with the fact that believers can "suffer LOSS" at the judgment. But it is one of the hard truths of God's Word (1 Cor. 3:11-15). What is that loss? Nearness to Christ in eternity. Those who shun His orders will never be close to Him in eternity. Why? There are no makeup classes in heaven. Nearness to Christ is reserved for those who mean business as His servants. So urgent is this truth that I have devoted an entire book to the matter. It is called JESUS IS COMING — GET READY CHRISTIAN! It stresses the fact that we have but one life in which to qualify ourselves for a place near Christ in heaven.

● Having said that, think back to the chapter that had to do with the Christian's private world. Think again how that is the world into which he is sent and the one for which he is responsible. Where will he account for that responsibility? At the Judgment. God never gives responsibility without also requiring accountability.

See now why I asked how many trips will a man make to gas stations during the rest of his life? How many phone booths will he pass? What will be the total of his trips to stores and shops? How many souls will he see on the job and at lunch? And how many times will Christian women visit markets, beauty shops, and department stores, to name but a few. In the course of their routines, Christians cross a multitude of people-paths. Their private worlds are laced with them. And most could be reached almost effortlessly—if they cared enough to bother.

Now that's what is going to come up at the Judgment Seat of Christ. The Lord will review the way each of us has carried out His orders to reach our private worlds. Our reward (or loss of reward) will be based on our obedience to His Commission. That's sobering, isn't it? See now why I have devoted my life to helping Christians reach their private worlds? I am determined to see that no brother or sister I can reach will have to feel ashamed in that day. If I can be used of God to make my eternal companions richer in heaven, my own joy will be that much greater in Christ.

> NOTE: When the truth of Christ's Lordship reaches down to a man's roots, He will serve the Master around the clock. When he goes to the store, for example, it will be to care for HIS business as well as buy groceries. This means witnessing for Jesus has the priority over shopping for food. When he wheels into the gas station it is no longer just to buy gas for his car, but to see if he can serve Christ in some way as well. His Master's wishes are uppermost in his mind. The same would be true of the Christian housewife. Her mind is not just occupied with, "Now we need this and that." She is also thinking, "How can I use this trip for Christ?" When the responsibility to reach our private world really grips us, that's the way our minds will work.

LET ME REPEAT MY EARLIER WARNING

I must pause for a moment to say something to those who will read this book and do nothing about the skills and actions described here. To them it is just good reading. In their minds they agree that the ladder is a terrific idea for God's people,

224

but they will not stir themselves to climb it. Right here I must say that such a thing is dangerous. . .

FOR IF YOU CAN

READ THIS BOOK AND DO NOTHING ABOUT IT,

SOMETHING IN YOU WILL DIE!

It mocks the Lord when He places such know-how as this in your hands only to have you ignore it. That's why I warned you not to read beyond page 58 unless you really meant business for Jesus. You are in a different position now than you were before you read this far. If we fail to heed the Lord when He speaks, His voice becomes weaker each time we shun His call.

You must not turn down the volume on Jesus by ignoring His plea to get going with the Great Commission. It is the clearest command in the New Testament. The next time He speaks, you will be less sensitive. Each time thereafter His voice will be fainter. That's what dies when we turn a deaf ear to the Holy Spirit. He is speaking to you now. I know it and you know it. So don't allow yourself to become immune to Christ.

If you haven't already done so, start up the ladder. Get that salvation letter off to me. There's an outline on page 243 that will help you write it. Within the covers of this book, the Lord has given you everything you need to be easy going and effective as a witness. You will find it joyous work once you acquire the skills, for they bring God's power into your life. Don't let anything stop you—neither the sneers of the world, your own timidities, or the deadening influence of inactive Christians. The churches are full of them. But you can overcome all this sluggishness in the Spirit's power.

● I don't like taking time out to repeat a warning, but it is timely after my mention of the Judgment Seat of Christ. And how does a man go about preparing himself for that judgment? By making a career of serving Christ. There is no finer way to advance that career than becoming serious about the Great Commission. The man who submits to Jesus' command to witness, will submit to His lordship in other areas of his life. Witnessing is by far the best place to begin. Why? Encouraging results come quickly. But there is no way to be a successful witness without becoming BUSINESS-LIKE about it.

SO GET BUSINESS-LIKE

You won't meet any advanced techniques in this chapter. This lesson is devoted to helping you become business-like in reaching your private world. You already have the skill. And now that you are at the top of the ladder, you know that it is possible for even the shiest Christian to reach his private world one way or another. All that remains is becoming business-like in obeying the Great Commission at your own strength-level.

This isn't a snap course, is it? Indeed not. It has taken you quite a while to get this far. Some of our correspondence course students take as long as three years to complete all ten steps. But that's okay. **Change** is the essence of this study, not time. You are not the same person who started up the ladder months ago. You are bolder. You are more at ease around people. Your personality has changed. You are more outgoing. You move with more grace and poise. You are of much greater credit to Christ. So it's worth it to take your time and allow CHANGES to occur in your person. Being a Christian witness is NOT just a matter of acquiring know-how. It has to do with revamping one's personality.

Now that you've reached the top, you are conscious of the Holy Spirit's power in your life. You know how to reach people. Does that mean you must now give the highest witness to every person you contact inside your private world? What a nightmare that would be. Your joy would vanish if you felt God required that. So relax. I have a surprise for you:

Even though you have climbed to the top of the ladder and own the sharpest witnessing skill available today, I want you to settle down in that level of witnessing which is the most comfortable for you.

Surprised?

It makes sense. The Lord expects us to be JOYOUS witnesses. Even as He expects us to be cheerful givers, so does He want us to be cheerful witnesses. Who can possibly be a cheerful witness if he feels obliged to extend himself beyond his natural strengths and abilities? It won't work and the Lord knows it. The ladder-method is His provision for the varying strengths in His people. He does NOT want any of us over-burdened. He said so:

"Take My yoke upon you. . .for My yoke is easy, and My burden is light" (Matt. 11:29,30).

WHY?

"The joy of the Lord is your strength" (Neh. 8:10).

Just as the Lord delights in cheerful givers, so does He desire joyous witnesses.

See now where I got the idea for WITNESSING MADE EASY? It was Jesus' idea. He gave it to me. The concept of making Christian work easier originated with our Lord. So somewhere among those ten rungs of the ladder is a witnessing level perfectly suited to your strengths. You may be one who is comfortable on rung no. 9. Fine, if you are. But again you may not be comfortable beyond rung no. 3. What is important is that you discover the type of witnessing that

227

gives you the most JOY as you serve the Lord. When you do, that's where I want you to settle down.

> NOTE: Does that mean you must never advance any higher? No. Anytime you find you can serve the Lord at a higher level, you will automatically advance yourself. That's why I had you go through all ten steps. You are familiar, at least with the whole range of witnessing action. From time to time you will find yourself experimenting with harder actions. As soon as you find you can do a harder witness comfortably, you'll move up. I've asked you to do assignments that may have been beyond you. But that was to acquaint you with the spectrum of witnessing. When it comes time for you to move up, you'll know what to do.

● After you settle down in your comfort level, you will be able to become business-like about reaching your private world. No longer will the type of witnessing concern you. Most of the threat will be gone as well. Then you will be free to focus on your career as a witness, that is, become business-like about it. So now we're ready for the question. . . "How does one go about becoming business-like as a witness for Christ?"

HE GETS ORGANIZED

You are headed for the store. I watch you come out of your house and head down the street. You have to be organized to do that. That's right. A person can't walk down the street without being organized. He has to put one foot down after another and keep them going in the right direction or he'll never reach his destination. So, even to go to the store, you have to plan the action and carry it out. Your feet must move in a series of controlled steps or you will never make it to the store.

If we have to be organized to get to the store, how much more do we need to be organized for the biggest work of our lives? Witnessing for Christ is the most important task we

228

have. I'm sure the Holy Spirit is bearing witness to that statement. If we need systematic action to reach the neighborhood market, do we need any less organization to carry out our work for Christ?

TAKE A LOOK AT YOUR DAY

As you look at the clock face, can you see any hour that doesn't belong to Jesus? We are His servants around the clock. But we sleep at night, you say. You're right, we can't witness when we're asleep. And in the early morning we're in such a rush to get to work, there's no way to witness then either. But what of the rest of the time? What of the daylight hours— driving to work, on the job, lunch, on the way home, the early evening? Shouldn't those hours be subject to His call? Of course. Those are our business hours, if we're in business for Christ. Those are the hours we must organize for the witnessing business.

PLANNING

1 Sit down at a table. Take out pencil and paper. Let a typical day pass before your imagination. As the day passes before your mind, think of those you contact frequently. If you made a list of them, it might include parking lot attendants, waitresses, office employees, gas station workers, car passengers, grocery clerks, maybe people at your club or at social gatherings. I mention those merely to stimulate your imagination. You may ride the bus for all I know and then there would be all those passengers.

> **NOTE: Many Christians move about within their private worlds and never see the people about them. That's because their minds are focused on themselves and restricted to personal matters. But the Lord Jesus wants us to have people-eyes. That's the kind He has. He sees people, for He is in the people-business. The Great Commission makes it your business too. Even though you are sitting at a table, picture those who cross your path during the day. See if you can't become people-conscious for a moment. Give thought to acquiring people-eyes. You're going to need them.**

2 On the left hand side of your paper provide for a column of names. Then, starting at the top of the sheet, make a list of the various people you might expect to meet during a typical day. Enter, for example, the words salesman or cab driver. If you are a housewife who doesn't get out much, your list would show the mailman or some salesperson who calls at the door. Those who report to work each day could have a longer list than someone who only gets out to shop one or two days a week. So, as you trace your steps throughout a day, write down in sequence those contacts that appear in your imagination. Leave room on the paper to rule four more columns.

SAMPLE "FIRE" CARD

PEOPLE	TRACT	WORDS & TRACT	WORDS ONLY	F-I-R-E
Elevator operator		✓		F E
Paper boy			✓	R E
Waitress	✓			E
gas attendant		✓		FIRE
Doctor			✓	F I
Cashier		✓		F I E
TOTAL				

231

❸ At the top of the first column write the word "People." At the head of the next column, enter the word "Tract." The third column should be labeled "Words and Tract," while the fourth column headed by "Words." At the top of the fifth column enter the letters F-I-R-E. They spell FIRE! You want to know about that "fire" don't you? It stands for the work of the Holy Spirit. As you do your witnessing, you will see Him do certain things for you. That column is reserved for putting down the work of the Spirit as it occurs in your witnessing. Each of the four letters stands for something He does for you as you deal with others.

"F"—When He grants you favor in the eyes of your prospect and it is obvious to you that He has done this, then write down the letter "F" in that column. It stands for favor.

"I"—When you notice you have seemingly invented a unique phrase right there on the spot, or have drastically altered the wording of anything I have supplied, and it comes off your lips with a strange freshness, enter the letter "I." It stands for inspiration.

"R"—When it is apparent your prospect is particularly impressed by your remarks, attaching serious weight to them, it is clear the Spirit has given you authority. This authority is prompting your prospect to show a marked respect for your words. Put down an "R" when you can see the Spirit causing your prospect to respect your ministry.

"E"—Do you find yourself enjoying unusual ease and relaxation as you speak to a prospect? Good. The Holy Spirit has done it. When your pulse no longer races and there is no struggle for words, this poise is the result of the Spirit's working. If you find you are not anxious to get away from the prospect, but actually enjoying yourself instead, this ease is from the Lord. Witnessing is a real delight when you can put down an "E" for ease.

When the Spirit of God gives you all those things in a single interview, you would mark down all four letters. . .FIRE. That will be some interview. In most cases, you will be able to write down one or more of those letters.

NOTE: I have already said much about the Holy Spirit as the basis for your confidence. Now you are going to have the splendid thrill of keeping track of the way He becomes your confidence. Your own spirit will rise as you see the record of His faithfulness to you. When you can enter FIRE after a name, regardless of the kind of a witness you use, the fire of God will burn in your soul. As you go on to build a history of moving in might, your life will take on a new glow. Your friends will notice the FIRE in your furnace. Nothing can stop it. Witnessing does that to God's people.

4 After you have made the list of people you could expect to meet in an average day, think next about the type of approach you might use with each one. If your actions are going to be limited to the lower rungs (1 to 3), then you will NOT be approaching anyone. You will be waiting for prospects to come to you. Your work will be limited to PASSIVE witnessing. But that's fine, if that is the limit of your ability to witness with JOY. I mean it when I say that Christians should work at their comfort level.

However, I would like to assume that every reader will be able to use his LIPS to make some form of an aggressive approach to the people on his list. And I am going to continue these instructions with that thought in mind. Even if one were to say nothing more than, "Did you notice my pin?"—it is an aggressive approach. It requires a response. So as you think through your list, think also of the phrases that would be natural for you to use. Don't pick out more than two or three, it's too hard to keep them on the tip of your tongue. Then write out the phrases you would use. Put them on cards so that you can carry them on your person.

5 Once you have your phrases on cards, practice with them before a mirror. It is best to do this when you are alone. You will feel foolish with your husband or wife watching you work on moves and expressions. Don't let Satan keep you from doing this. The technique is terrific for helping you to be pressure-free in actual situations. The relaxation you feel as you do this before a mirror will "carry over" when you witness in a live situation. If you do this in simulated actions enough times, the transfer of nervous and mental ease will be astonishing. You will be relaxed.

> **NOTE: People do not experience the best learning under crisis conditions. A man might learn to "swim" by being thrown into a pool. That is, the desperation of his situation might generate enough power for him to "swim" to safety. He'd have to learn to "swim" to save himself. But he will never become a good swimmer. Why? The crude stroke learned in the crisis will be difficult to get rid of. And so it is with the witness who learns in crises only. On the other hand, if he can acquire moves and self-expression in the stress-free privacy of his bedroom, polished witnessing will fix itself in his personality and carry over to the actual situation. The relaxation does carry over, as any golfer, rifleman, or actor will testify.**

So with that much preparation you're ready to go.

ASSIGNMENT

For your last assignment, I will ask you to organize your life around the command of Christ for one week. That is, for a period of seven days, the Great Commission will have the priority. Witnessing will be your chief business as you go about your normal routine. I emphasize the word "normal." I do NOT want you to go out of your way to make contacts. That would spoil the assignment. I mean for you to become business-like about reaching those who paths you ordinarily cross as you live out an average week.

The only way to face up to the gap in our lives is to take a week and devote it solidly to the job the Lord has given us. You will be surprised to discover how little any of us really devotes to the Lord's business. The contrast you experience between a dedicated week and a casual week may shock you. We really do put ourselves first most of the time. Jesus gets a crumb now and then and that's about all.

You may like the new life. You may just revel in the Spirit's presence as you put Christ first and not wish to return to the old life at the end of the week. We'll see. It will be the actual DOING that tells the story. There's no way to speculate about it. In any event, make witnessing your business for one week and see what it does for your life. The least that can happen is that you will want to be more systematic about serving the Lord than you were before. All right, we've talked enough. It's time for you to move out. Go about it like this:

1. Start on a Monday morning so that your seven days are finished by Sunday night. As you are about to leave your house, set your spirit, "God helping me, this week is going to be devoted to the Great Commission. I am going to make it MY BUSINESS to take advantage of the opportunities that come to me this day and witness for Jesus!"

2. Don't allow fears to pile up in advance of doing this assignment. If you do, you'll be worrying about things that will not happen. If you have to be fearful, wait until the actual moment arrives. Then you can be as scared as you want. But it won't matter then. You will have reached the point when the Holy Spirit rushes to arm you with His presence. If you hesitate to do this assignment out of fear of what people might think, that will be Satan's doing.

REMEMBER: Christian courage is not the absence of fear, but conquering it through developing an awareness of the Holy Spirit's presence. It takes some fear to make witnessing an adventure, as is also true in many sporting events.

3. Keep a record of your interviews.

Have you noticed how the Highway Patrolman sits in his car making out a report after citing a motorist? You should do the same. After your prospect has departed, pause a moment to jot down what took place. Under the anointing some nice things may come off your lips, or some unique way to exploit the situation may have developed. One day, when you are teaching this skill to others, these will be among your treasures. They are too precious to lose.

235

4. Keep in motion. Be serious about your witnessing business for the seven days. Don't slacken after the 3rd or 4th day. Work hard for one week. Keep watching for people. As serious as you are, be sure to maintain your joy. Be enthusiastic. Keep that smile in place. You are operating at your comfort level, now, not some advanced step. Stay close to the Holy Spirit and He will transform you into a bouyant and warm personality.

5. Then Sunday comes—seven days later. Early that morning look at the record. See what God has done through you? That will put a song in your heart. When you get to church, your heart will be full of excitement. If your church allows testimonies, be ready to get to your feet and tell the people what it means to have a week of witnessing under your belt. I mean a week of making witnessing your chief business. The people will feel the excitement. They'll respond to your enthusiasm. They will sense that not the half of it has been told.

HINT: PC has available a booklet called 'Witnessing Is My Business." It is designed for recording the highlights of your witnessing interviews. There is room for dates and places and details for at least 20 interviews. A week in the witnessing business should fill the booklet. Have it in your hand when you get up to testify. Hold it up for all to see: "This book is titled 'Witnessing Is My Business.' It contains the record of what the Holy Spirit and I have been doing together this week as we witnessed for Christ." Then, using the information in your hands, share one or two outstanding incidents with the people. It's hard to remember all that happens in this business, so it can be helpful to have such a record.

6. When the week is over, you will be finished with the entire study. You will have climbed the ladder and be on your way as a lifetime witness. It is possible that the one week devoted to the witnessing business will settle it for you. You may decide it should have the priority from now on. If so, you will become a professional Christian, a full-time worker for Christ. Full time, you recall, does not mean working for a Christian organization. It means serving CHRIST full time. It has nothing to do with how you earn your living.

HINT: Professional people use business cards. If you elect to make witnessing your business, you may wish to use some of the witnessing business cards produced by Personal Christianity. A PC business card not only gives your name and address, it also carries a testimony. (See sample below). The cards have space on the front where your local printer can imprint your name and address. Then it can be used in place of an ordinary business card. Offering one of these cards, after you have given some kind of a witness, carries a lot of wallop for Christ.

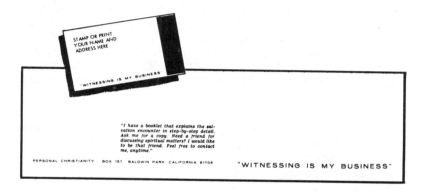

STAMP OR PRINT YOUR NAME AND ADDRESS HERE

"WITNESSING IS MY BUSINESS"

"I have a booklet that explains the salvation encounter in step-by-step detail. Ask me for a copy. Need a friend for discussing spiritual matters? I would like to be that friend. Feel free to contact me, anytime."

PERSONAL CHRISTIANITY   BOX 157   BALDWIN PARK, CALIFORNIA 91706

"WITNESSING IS MY BUSINESS"

My Business. . . !

Like you, I work for a living. But my real business is telling people about Christ — not as a religion, but as a living Person ready to save people from hell! True, it's your own business what you do about that, but seeing that you hear His offer to enter your heart and life, is mine.

His invitation reads: "Behold I stand at the door and knock: if any man hear my voice and open the door, I **will come in. . .**" (Rev. 3:20).

Just as you would open the door of your home to a friend's knock, so can you open your heart to Christ. Pray: "Come into my heart Lord and make yourself real to me." He will — in**stantly!** You'll know your sins are forgiven and you're ready to meet God. Then you'll be glad this is. . . . **My business!**

7. Think about passing the skill on to others. By the time you finish this study, you will know a lot about the witnessing business. Too much, in fact, to keep to yourself. There are many around you who know almost nothing. You don't have to be a gifted teacher to share this skill. You have the best qualification of all—experience. In addition, PC can supply tools and aids for non-teachers to begin a witnessing class in any church or group.

SUCCESS MOTIVATION

"Nothing succeeds like success!" You've heard that before. It's true, too. As you read this book, did you wonder if the Ladder-Method was really successful, that it really does what I promise? Let me say this; the plan for lifting shy Christians from silence to outspoken witnessing for Christ is extremely successful. Many have climbed the ladder and their changed lives are the "proof of the pudding." Whole churches have come alive as the people recovered the thrill of Christ through witnessing.

But of course you would expect me to say that. Well, you don't have to take my word for it. A mountain of letters has come to us from grateful people telling what this witnessing course has done in their lives. I'm going to let you read a few. It's all right. I have their permission to share these letters with you. The writers are graduates of the correspondence course and most eager to have their testimonies encourage others for Jesus.

● **"I shall be eternally grateful. . .!"**

Dear C. S.:

I shall be eternally grateful to the Lord for using you and the "Ladder-Method" to finally motivate me to satisfy a deep, years' long need to become obedient to the Great Commission. I joyfully anticipate going on from here into the soul-winning ministry. I can't put into words how grateful I am for the day I got on your mailing list and was introduced to this course. If I don't see you in this life to thank you, I'll see you in glory!

Paul F. Sinclair
7 Rockland Rd.
Trenton, NJ 86838

- **"I couldn't have continued in His plan. . .!"**

Dear Brother Lovett:

Words cannot express my appreciation for the knowledge and skill I have received through this witnessing course. I only know the Holy Spirit has done this for me through you. I don't see how His plan for my life could have been carried out without it. But now He has provided it through you, praise the Lord.

Marvin E. Hanneman
2195 Orchard Lane
Merced, CA 95340

- **"I experience His presence and power more. . .!"**

Dear C.S.:

This course has taught me the workings of the blessed Holy Spirit so that I experience His presence and power more in my life. It has given me the tools and know-how I needed to get the message to people. I would not have been able to do my work for Him without it. Thank God for you, CS, and the staff at PC. I pray for you daily. PS: I am presently teaching a class of 14 students the "easy" way to witness!

Paul Singrey
937 Taylor
Elkart, IN 46514

- **"We are both having real thrills. . .!"**

Dear Brother:

I can hardly believe the change that has occurred in me and my husband since taking this course together. We are both having real thrills in witnessing together. I have been a Christian for many years and have distributed many tracts, but never by such methods and with such reliance on the Holy Spirit for results! I now experience a new awareness of the presence of Christ!

Mrs. Mae McKee
310 E. Main St.
Bradford, PA 16701

- **"I experienced the marvelous power of the Holy Spirit!"**

Dear Friends at PC:

My ministry has just begun! I'll never be the same again! Never in my Christian life have I experienced the marvelous power of the Holy Spirit as I do today! He is more than a doctrine to me now. He is my business Partner and the President of our team. If only other brethren knew what would happen to them if they had this know-how power in witnessing. The whole world would be turned upside down for Jesus. I can't praise God enough for bringing this course into my life. I'm ready to go on to soul-winning now. God bless you.

Keith H. Whiteman
371 Walnut St.
Pottstown, PA 19464

- **"I have never seen anything as effective. . .!"**

Dear Brother:

I have never seen anything anywhere as effective as the "Ladder-Method" for getting silent Christians to become vocal for Christ. I really took this course so that I could teach it to others. But I was amazed at the way I was letting opportunities slip by me in my normal daily routine. I have won souls, but oh how fear controlled me. Now, through taking this course, I am over-coming fear and making each day count for Christ!

Tom F. Brown
438 Sylvia St.
Encinitas, CA 92024

- **"Witnessing has become natural. . .!"**

Dear C. S.:

This course has transformed my life. Through the Holy Spirit, witnessing has become natural in my life instead of something like a cloak that I would put on from time to time. I am sharing my witnessing experiences and joy with others. I'm sure you are going to hear from many, for I find that there are Christians who really want to know how to witness for Christ.

Elbert H. Bolsen
Rt 4, Box 160
Warrensburg, MO 64093

● "This course has given me a goal. . ."

Dear Brother Lovett:

When I became a Christian three years ago, I purposed to be a faithful witness for the Lord Jesus. Now God has used your gifted teaching methods to direct and build up my witness to accomplish this desire. Also, learning to witness in the power of the Holy Spirit has led me into soul-winning situations. Because of this, I have had the joy of leading many friends and acquaintances to Christ.

Mrs. Stephen E. Jordan
Rt 4, Box 340 Amsterdam Rd.
Scotia, NY 12302

● "It has armed me. . .!"

Dear Dr. Lovett:

Words cannot express what this course has done for me. With it, the Holy Spirit has armed me with so much to use for the Lord. Also, it finally got me into soul-winning. Your book, SOUL-WINNING MADE EASY, opened the door to that field for me. Today I had four teen-agers with me. They were all unsaved, but I was able to lead one of them to Christ. Pray that I might be able to win the other three also. Oh, the field is white unto the harvest. May the Lord use me to gather part of it for Him!

C. R. Snelgrove
PO Box 551
Jefferson, TX 75657

ISN'T THAT SOMETHING!

Did you notice how all those graduates testified to the Holy Spirit's power in their lives? They were quick to acknowledge that HE, not C. S. Lovett, was the One Who brought this course into their lives and changed them. That makes it of God. That is also why I dare to boast in the Lord of what the Ladder-Method can do for His people. I'm not bragging about myself, but the Holy Spirit Who works through me.

Jonathan Goforth tells of the woodpecker who lit on a tree and took three pecks at the mighty trunk. Just then thunder rolled across the sky. A storm was brewing. The crashing sound scared the woodpecker away. While he was gone, lightning struck and shattered the tree. When all quieted down, the little bird returned and surveyed the damage.

"My my," he said, **"Just three little pecks and look what I did!"**

Well, lightning does strike when we move in God's power. But we know Who really does the work. In that, we're wiser than the woodpecker. A proper attitude is that of the little boy whose dad just knocked the ball out of the park. . . "That's my dad!" It's good for Christians to be proud of the Holy Spirit. So when we brag, we brag about Him. After all. . .

HE IS WONDERFUL!

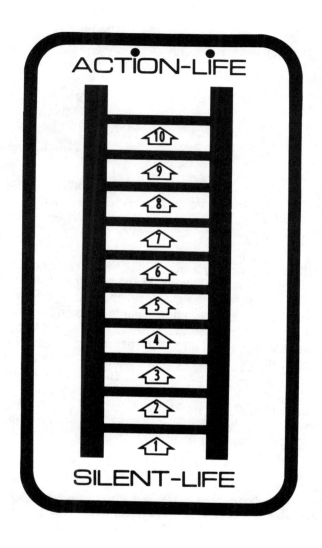

BECOMING A WITNESS IS EASIER—ONE STEP AT A TIME.

IF YOU WANT TO TAKE
THE WITNESSING COURSE
BY CORRESPONDENCE

You can take the course from **PERSONAL CHRIST-
IANITY** with me as your personal coach.   All ten lessons of the ladder-method have been prepared as a correspondence course.

NOTE: Let me way a word about the correspondence
course. It is NOT a pencil/paper type. It is an
ACTION course. There are specific witnessing actions you are to do, all of them in the same vein as
the one I described above. After you do these actions you send me an action report. There is one for
each of the 10 rungs of the ladder. You will NOT
receive all ten lessons at once. You will receive two
lessons at first. Then, as soon as I receive your first
action report, the next lesson is mailed to you. That
way you always have one lesson to work on while
the other is in the mail.

There are three things to do to enroll in the course:

1. Find the application form, p. 249. Read it and fill it out. Sign it. From
the information on this application a permanent record is made for you here
at PC headquarters and a chart is used to plot your progress.

2. Sit down and write a letter to me telling how you KNOW you are saved.
I want you to put your salvation experience on paper. To do so, ask yourself . . . **"What right do I have to call myself a born-again Christian?"** Think
too about the ways you reassure yourself you are safe in the Lord. Put it all

on paper, describing the best you can the mechanics of your surety in Christ. It doesn't have to be long, just factual. I am not interested in your spelling or handwriting.

Don't try to satisfy me with your statement, satisfy yourself.

This action is not as simple as it sounds. To put things of this nature on paper, a person must first process them in his mind. It often takes a lot of mental energy to reshape scattered and unfocused ideas into a solid statement, but that's what I want. If your experience in Christ is vague and shadowy, this can be a rewarding assignment. The witness-life requires a firm base. It is the launching pad from which you will go into orbit, so it must be solid.

3.   Along with your application and salvation letter, enclose the enrollment fee. This fee covers the complete cost of all materials used in climbing the witnessing ladder. Your investment in this course will reap great reward in heaven. The purpose of this course is solely to activate saints for Christ, with the confidence that our "profit" will be laid up and waiting for the day when we will see you there!

Here are the advantages of climbing the witnessing ladder this way:

- Your work is more determined and systematic with the discipline of accounting to someone else, as reinforced by the heart-treasure principle when you invest the $20.00.

- If you are a pastor or teacher, you can systematically bring your people along a step or two behind you. You can put the know-how to work in your group even as you ascend the 10 rungs of the ladder.

- Each time we receive an action report, you receive a prayer-boost by name as your report goes before the Friday night prayer-band.

- If you begin to show excessive lag in your reporting, a follow-up letter will spur you on to increased dedication.

- You receive a membership card and **permanent number** when you reach the fifth rung of the ladder. This number can be used to earn an **immediate discount** on all supplies you order from PC. In time this can return the cost of the course.

- Upon completion of the course, you receive the silver PC pin. These coveted pins are kept locked in a safe, and there is no way to secure one except by completing all ten action steps of the witnessing ladder. They truly certify the wearer to be an active and skilled witness for Christ.

- You can take your time. Some take as long as one year to complete the course. The fastest is three months. You advance to the next higher rung after you have learned to be **comfortable** witnessing at the lower level. The pressure is your own ambition to go as far as you can in Christ.

Go to the place where you do your letter writing. Take pen and paper and get your salvation experience down in black and white. You'll enjoy sweet exhilaration doing just that much. There's a sample letter on page 248 that can serve as a guide if letter writing is hard for you. Now Satan wants you to put this off. Don't listen to him. The Holy Spirit is ready to work with you right now. As soon as you get that letter on its way to me, your faith will begin to rise. Get started as a witness and you will discover the. . .

REAL THRILL OF CHRIST!

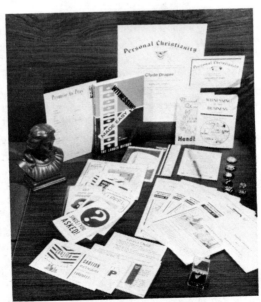

Here are some of the items in the "Witnessing Course by Correspondence."

How to get started

1. Fill out the application on page 249.
2. Prepare the statement of your salvation experience. Sample letter on next page.
3. Enclose your check or money order.
4. Expect your first lesson in about 2 weeks.

We furnish everything

COMPLETE COST $20.00

This includes:

☆ Copy of your text WITNESSING MADE EASY
☆ Assorted tracts for assignments
☆ Witness pins
☆ Witnessing pen and DASH WARNING SIGN
☆ Pocket plastic tract holder
☆ Booklets and dailog cards
☆ Lesson sheets and action report forms
☆ Maintenance of your individual file
☆ Lifted to Jesus by name in prayer group
☆ Completion certificate and silver PC pin
☆ Numbered membership card giving you 10% discount on purchases at PC after fourth lesson report is completed.

Graduation means

● You have traveled from silence to outspokenness for Christ

● You have learned the skill of working with the Holy Spirit

● You have learned how to create a witnessing situation

● You have overcome fear and embarrassment by action

SAMPLE LETTER

Date ————————————

Dear "C. S."

I have been reading **WITNESSING MADE EASY** and I want to be a witness for our Lord Jesus.

And here is my experience in Christ:
"I know that I am saved because..."

INSTRUCTIONS

Complete your letter in a paragraph or two and don't worry about the following:

1. Spelling
2. Handwriting, though I do have to read it. Typewriter would be helpful if you have one.
3. Grammar or sentence structure
4. Lack of education
5. What I think of the letter as to style. I am interested only in your experience.

HINTS

1. Do you have a favorite text on which you rest your salvation?
2. Is there a date or event which you can recall when you opened your heart to Jesus?
3. Are there ways in which you reestablish your heart when doubts strike?
4. Review in your mind the actual transaction which takes place when one receives the Lord. Can you mention something of the mechanics?

I am glad we can become personal friends, brother Lovett. And I look forward to receiving the coaching helps. I will be faithful to ask the Holy Spirit to work with us on this program and help me to become a vigorous witness for our Lord Jesus as the know-how comes into my life.

Eagerly in Christ,

Signed ————————————————————

WITNESSING COURSE
BY CORRESPONDENCE
APPLICATION

photo or
snapshot
if
available

PERSONAL CHRISTIANITY
Box 549
Baldwin Park, CA 91706 (818) 338-7333

Date_____

Name_____

Address_____

City_____

State & Zip_____

Minister __ Teacher __ Layman __ Housewife __ Student __

Name of your church_____

Your Occupation_____

Do you receive a copy of Dr. Lovett's MARANATHA FAMILY Mini-Magazine monthly?_____

I want to be a witness for our Lord Jesus. I hereby apply for the action course you offer. Enclosed is $20.00 to cover the cost of the lessons and materials needed for the assignments.

Check one below:

My salvation experience letter is enclosed_____

You already have my salvation letter_____

CLIP HERE AND MAIL THIS PORTION

No. 102

No. 104

FOR THE TEACHER

No. 102 ■ TEACH WITNESSING (Teacher's Guide for WITNESSING MADE EASY) — By C. S. Lovett

(book size 5¼" x 8¼", shrinkwrapped)

You may begin teaching right after you yourself have started up the witnessing ladder, but you must be far enough along so that your teaching bears the authority of experience and you radiate the confidence that comes with discovering the Holy Spirit's power to cancel fear!

Paperback, 240-page teacher's text filled with photos, dialogues, simulated situations sets forth every detail for an action class in witnessing. It covers a period of 13 weeks allowing time for students to carry out their assignments and enjoy critique-report sessions in class. Also it fits the church's calendar quarter so that the sessions may be inserted into the Sunday school program without disturbing the overall teaching plan.

No. 104 ■ WITNESSING CLASS TEACHER'S PACKET — By C. S. Lovett

The teacher's kit lets you examine all of the materials you'll be using even as you are studying the teacher's text. It's much easier to plan out a class-session when you have the tools and helps in your hands. Not only is preparation easier, but it is simpler to develop publicity announcing your classes. These classes are recommended for 9th graders on up, and can be taught in church, home or any group.

Includes poster, badge, and signs needed as teacher's props not included in 5-STUDENT UNIT.

No. 135

TOOLS FOR YOUR CLASS

No. 135 ■ WITNESSING CLASS 5-STUDENT UNIT (without WITNESSING MADE EASY student texts)

Everything you need to teach a class as outlined in TEACH WITNESSING.

Contains all the material each student will need for the entire 13 week class.

Teachers order 1 unit for every 5 students.

(Does not include teacher's props. These are included in No. 104 WITNESSING CLASS TEACHER'S PACKET. Does not include WITNESSING MADE EASY students texts which are sold separately.)

EACH 5-STUDENT UNIT CONTAINS:

TRACTS

50 Religion Can Be Dangerous, 25 Here's A Tip On Life, 25 Bills Bills Bills, 25 Owe A Letter, 100 Since You Asked, 50 Would You Be Embarrassed, 5 Get Wise Witness, 50 Wisest Man In The World, 5 Thank You

BOOKLETS
5 Witnessing Is My Business
5 Your Biggest Decision

PINS
5 Question Mark, 5 Ask Me, 5 Owl

CARDS
5 Poemcards, 5 Challenge/Follow-Up, 5 Prayer Commitment, 5 Mid-Week Thank You

FOLDERS
5 Witnessing Class Workshop, 5 Witnessing Correspondence Course Application

OTHER
5 Supreme Court Decision Slips, 5 Plastic Pocket Tract Holders, 3 F-E-A-R Slips, 5 sets of Witnessing Class Report Forms, 5 Witnessing Class Award Certificates

FRAMING THE REPRODUCTION OF THE CRUCIFIXION

© LINDA LOVETT 1971

The 16" X 20" reproduction of the oil painting, **"It Is Finished!"** comes rolled in a mailing tube. As soon as it arrives, open the package carefully and then place the reproduction where it can stretch out. Be sure it is out of reach of little fingers. The size will provide you with a picture in your home that is big enough to attract attention, yet one for which it is easy to secure a frame. It is a standard frame size.

You can frame the reproduction yourself. Check with the department and variety stores for a dark wood frame with a light color liner. That combination makes the colors stand out best. Then secure some artist's board or other heavy material on which to mount the reproduction. To fasten the reproduction to the board, use spray-on adhesive. Do not use liquid glue. It lumps and the spots will show through the reproduction. After the reproduction is fixed on the artist's board, then you can insert it into the frame.

If you are not fairly good with your hands, we recommend that you have your reproduction mounted for you in a frame shop. Most places will do the whole job for around $10.00 or less. This painting is going to serve the Lord and grace your home for many years, so it is worth the extra cost to see that it is mounted properly. You are going to be thrilled with the way it turns your home into a witness every time you have visitors.

"IT IS FINISHED!" (Crucifixion of Jesus) **full color reproduction of an original oil painting by Linda Lovett**

No. 134 (UNFRAMED

(Each reproduction comes with 10 No. 437 **RIDDLE OF THE CROSS** tracts and instructions, and gold title sticker)

252

MEET THE MARANATHA MAN!

Now that you have read **WITNESSING MADE EASY** and sensed its power through the Holy Spirit, would you like to know more about the author? Would you like to know what makes C. S. Lovett tick; what God has called him to do and why? Then you will want to read his autobiography . . . **MARANATHA MAN!**

No. 548 ■ **C. S. LOVETT: MARANATHA MAN**
An autobiography

Thrill to the story of a man who was raised without father or mother — kidnapped for a year — became a gun-toting gang leader and almost a murderer at 14 — a death defying World War II pilot — building a financial empire after the war and giving his fortune away after God became his Father — and how God molded him into a godly servant whose writings have changed countless lives for Christ.

When you see that all he had going for him was yieldedness to Jesus, you'll say to yourself, "If God can do that for him, He can do it for me!" And when you behold the vision God has given him, preparing the "bride of Christ" for Jesus' appearing, and how easy it is for you to get in on it — you'll want to become a MARANATHA MAN or MARANATHA WOMAN yourself!

No. 428 HOW TO GET RID OF RELIGIOUS
FANATICS Tract

No. 406 WHAT TO DO IN CASE I VANISH Tract

No. 413 SINCE YOU ASKED Tract
No. 475 QUESTION MARK Pin
No. 476 ASK ME! Pin

No. 426 CURIOUS? Tract

No. 401 THE RIDDLE OF THE CROSS Tract

No. 414 THE WISEST MAN IN THE WORLD Tract

No. 420 GET WISE—WITNESS! Tract
No. 478 OWL Pin

No. 416 A PENNY FOR YOUR THOUGHTS Tract
No. 477 1¢ Pin

No. 422 I FEEL GREAT! Tract

No. 407 WOULD YOU BE EMBARRASSED? Tract

No. 402 HERE'S A TIP ON LIFE Tract

No. 411 THANK YOU Tract

No. 403 BILLS, BILLS, BILLS Tract

No. 404 OWE A LETTER? Tract

No. 408 CAUTION RELIGION CAN BE DANGEROUS

These items and free catalog of all Dr. Lovett's
works are available from:

PERSONAL CHRISTIANITY
Box 549, Baldwin Park, CA 91706
helping Christians "prepare for His appearing" since 1951